Caribbean Soul
Vegan & Vegetarian Cookbook

Also by Firehorse Entertainment

Goodbye Money Pie
So Hear Me All
Gems
Viva Las Vegan
Diving for the Cross
Even the Moon
Set Etiquette

For more information, visit www.FirehorseEnt.com

Caribbean Soul

Vegan & Vegetarian Cookbook

DL Phelps

FIREHORSE ENTERTAINMENT
St. Petersburg & San Francisco
2018

FIREHORSE ENTERTAINMENT, LLC
St. Petersburg & San Francisco
www.FirehorseEnt.com

©2018 by DL Phelps
All rights reserved. No part of this book may be reproduced in any form or by any means, electronic or mechanical, including photocopying, recording, or by any information storage and retrieval system, without permission in writing from the publisher.

First Edition
PRINTED IN THE UNITED STATES OF AMERICA
The Library of Congress catalogs the trade paperback edition of the book as follows:

Phelps, DL
Caribbean Soul; Vegan & Vegetarian Cookbook.
 I. Authorship. I. Title.
KDP ISBN- 9781723775222
2017 CreateSpace print version ISBN-9781982090562

Copyright © 2017 DL Phelps. All rights reserved.

Editor: Valerie Kalfrin

Photo credits:
Front cover: DL Phelps
Back cover: DL Phelps

Caribbean Soul

Vegan & Vegetarian
Cookbook

By
DL Phelps

Forward

Who loves food? Food not only nourishes our bodies and feeds our minds its' full of mystery and delight, history and traditions. My first memories of the delights the Caribbean had to offer happened when I was a kid in Puerto Rico. I'll never forget sitting in the restaurant in San Juan and seeing the elaborate selection of vegetarian dishes offered. Then to be served black beans and rice like it was the most celebrated exalted food there was, truly left an impression on me. The flavors of the islands seeped into my soul. A fresh cut pineapple that you eat right out of the skin. Mangos so sweet and juicy you can't even cut the flesh. Your left with only juice and what else can you do? But add some local rum and make the freshest Mango Daiquiris.

On a recent trip to the Bahamas, while on beach at Clifton plantation my crew and I enjoyed a famously traditional meal of peas n rice, baked mac and cheese and fried plantains. The meal included broiled snapper and bbq chicken but these flavors can easily be replicated with vegetarian options that will transport you to the islands.

In support of a vegetarian lifestyle is the ethical treatment of animals raised for food products. Research your food sources and whenever possible support your local organic farmers! Shopping locally supports your neighbors, and communities. My passion for vegan meat-free dishes continues and I hope you enjoy the delicious dishes collected here.

People will always gather where there is good food, good friends and love. The most important ingredient in any dish is the love; don't forget to put in the love. Wishing you all the best. Namaste'

May you be truly blessed,

DL Phelps
St. Petersburg, 2018

Contents

Caribbean Soul

1. Cocktails 14
   - Always Sunny Never Scurvy, Martini
   - Bahamian Sky Juice
   - Banana and Papaya Smoothie (Non-Alcoholic)
   - Blue Moon over Miami Martini
   - Coconut and Mango Smoothie (Non-Alcoholic)
   - Cuba-Cranny
   - Daiquiri (Mango, Banana, Pineapple, Peach, Frozen)
   - Dark & Stormy
   - Ginger Beer (Non-Alcoholic)
   - Guava and Lime Juice (Non-Alcoholic)
   - Hail Miami Mary
   - Key Lime Margarita
   - Key Lime Pie Cocktail
   - Mojito
   - Pina Colada
   - Planter's Punch
   - Ponche de Crème (Trinidad's Christmas drink)
   - Rum Punch
   - Simple Syrup
   - South Beach Sunrise
   - Ting with a Sting
   - Welcome to the Island Drink

2. Appetizers 28
   - Akkra Bean Fritters
   - Artichoke Leek Frittata
   - Cassava Chips
   - Coconut Roasted Bananas
   - Empanadas
   - Fritters
   - Ginger Beer Roasted Pineapple
   - Mofongo Plantain Spread
   - Phulouri Split Pea Fritters
   - Picklises
   - Platanutri Plantain Chips
   - Sweet Potato Chips
   - Tostones de Platano, Green Plantain Chips

3. Soups & Stews 43
   - Black Bean Soup - Trini Style
   - Callaloo Soup
   - Chili, Jamaican Me Crazy - Jamaica
   - Corn Soup - Trini Style
   - Groundnut Soup – St. Kitts
   - Lentil Soup

- Mushroom Barley Soup
- Okra & Tomato Stew
- Pepperpot Apple's Antiqua
- Pepperpot Jamaican Soup
- Pepperpot Antiquan
- Picadillo Crockpot
- Pumpkin Soup - Jamaica
- Red Pea Stew – Jamaica
- Veggie Burger Chowder – Bermuda

4. Sauces 60
    - Coconut and Sage Carmel Sauce - Jamaica
    - Coconut Sauce - Jamaica
    - Creole Sauce - Trinidad
    - Habanero Lime Butter Sauce - Jamaica
    - Jerk Rub - Jamaica
    - Mango Chutney - Jamaica
    - Mango Jam - Jamaica
    - Pepper Wine - Jamaica
    - Pickled Scotch Bonnet Peppers / Homemade Pickapep - Jamaica
    - Pineapple Jam - Jamaica
    - Pineapple Sauce – Jamaica
    - Salsa Rojo para Frijoles Negros, *Sweet Pepper Sauce for Black Beans* – Cuba
    - Sauce Vinaigrette, *French Dressing* – French Islands
    - Sofrito - Cuba

5. Grain & Pasta Dishes 76
    - Akee Patties – Jamaica
    - Almond Milk Rice – Jamaica
    - Arroz Blanco, White Rice – Dominican republic
    - Arroz con Ajo, Garlic Rice – Cuba
    - Arroz con frijoles, Rice with Beans – Dominican republic
    - Baked Mac and Cheese - Bahamian
    - Beans and Rice, Jamaican Style
    - Congis, Red Beans and Rice - Cuba
    - Dal, Split Pea or Lentil Puree – Trinidad
    - Frijoles Negros Pascuales, Holiday Black Beans – Cuba
    - Frijoles Negros, Black Beans – Cuba
    - Kwaku's Fungi
    - Peas and Rice, Bahamian Style
    - Pois et Riz Colles, Rice and Beans Together – Haiti
    - Pois et Riz, Peas and Rice – Guadeloupe
    - Rice and Peas – Jamaica
    - Rice and Pumpkin - Jamaica
    - Riz a l'aubergine, Rice with Eggplant - Haiti
    - Riz au Djon-Dijon, Rice with Black Mushrooms – Haiti
    - Riz Creole, Rice Creole Style – Martinique-Guadeloupe

6. Vegetables & Salad Dishes 99
    - Ackee Souffle – Jamaica
    - Acrates d'aubergine, *Eggplant Fritters* – Martinique-Guadeloupe

- Acrates de chou palmist, *Palm Heart Fritters* – Martinique-Guadeloupe
- Alu Talkari, *Potato Curry* – Trinidad
- Asparagus Pudding – US Virgin Islands
- Aubergine a la Tomate, *Eggplant with Tomatoes* – Martinique
- Baked Pawpaw, *Papaya* – Jamaica
- Banane jaune avec sauce blanche, *Green Bananas with white sauce* – Martinique
- Berehein na forno, *Eggplant in Coconut Cream* – St. Maarten
- Breadfruit COO-COO – Barbados
- Breadfruit stuffed with Ackee – Jamaica
- Cassava Coo-Coo – Windward Islands
- Chou Palmiste en Sauce Blanche, *Palm Hearts in White Sauce* - – Martinique-Guadeloupe
- Christohene au Gratin, *Chayote with Cheese and Onion Stuffing* – Martinique
- Colombo de Giraumon, *Pumpkin Curry* – Martinique-Guadeloupe
- Concombre en Daube, *Stewed Cucumbers* – Martinique
- Concombres en Salade, *Cucumber Salad* – Martinique
- Conquintay coo-coo – Trinidad
- COO-COO
- Coo-Coo – Barbados
- Coo-Coo – Tobago
- Corn and Coconut Coo-Coo - Grenada
- Curried Vege Chunks
- Daube de Giraumon, *Seasoned West Indian Pumpkin* – Martinique-Guadeloupe
- Foo-Foo, *Pounded Green Plantain Balls* – Trinidad-Barbados
- Fried Okras – Jamaica
- Fried Ripe Plantains – All Islands
- Fruit Salad cups with lemon, mango and mint - Bahamas
- Funchi – *Corn Meal Pudding* – Netherlands Antilles
- Giraumon Boulli, *Boiled West Indian Pumpkin* – Martinique-Guadeloupe
- Key Lie Honey Salad Dressing
- Key West Spinach & Jackfruit Salad
- La Salade de Leyritz, *Salad Leyritz* – Northern Martinique
- Matete de Fruit a Pain, *Sauted Breadfruit* – Guadeloupe
- Moros y Cristianos, *Moors and Christians* - Cuba
- Okra in Tomato Sauce – St. Croix
- Palm Heart & Papaya Salad - Caribbean
- Pepino en Salsa de Naranja, *Stewed Cucumbers in Orange Sauce* – Puerto Rico
- Quingombos Guisados, Stewed Okra – Puerto Rico
- Ratatouille Creole – Guadeloupe
- Roasted Breadfruit – Jamaica
- Sautéed Cabbage – Jamaica
- Steamed Callaloo – Jamaica
- Stuffed Cho-Cho, Chayote - Jamaica
- Stuffed Pawpaw, Papaya – Jamaica
- Sweet Corn Coo-Coo – Trinidad
- Sweet Potato Salad - Caribbean
- Temphe Pasta Salad - Caribbean

- Watercress Salad – Jamaica

7. Breakfast Dishes 152
    - Corn and Potato Cakes - Mexico
    - Curried Tofu Scramble - Florida
    - Good Morning Sunshine Frittata - Florida
    - Herbed Avocado Toast - Florida
    - Oatmeal with Cinnamon Sugar and Pecans - Florida
    - Oven Roasted Potato with Rosemary - Florida
    - Pineapple Papaya Salad with Dried Apricots & Coconut - Cuba
    - Rice Porridge with Gingered Blueberries and Toasted Nuts - Cayman
    - Savory Porridge with Vegetable –Trinidad

8. Main Dishes 163
    - Easy Soy Milk – DIY
    - Easy Tofu - DIY
    - Bahamian Style Grilled LOST HER
    - Bahamian MA UNHI
    - Jerked LOST HER with Coconut
    - Grilled SALM - UN with Habanero Lime Butter
    - Grilled Spiny LOST HER with Basil Butter
    - Margarita MA UNHI Acapulco
    - CrockPot Jerk Tofu
    - Grilled Tofu with Fresh Mango Salsa
    - Lechon Asado: Cuban Shredded Jackfruit

9. Breads & Puddings 181
    - Banana and Corn Meal Festival - Jamaica
    - Coconut and Sweet Potato Pudding - Jamaica
    - Coconut Johnny Cake – All Islands
    - Fried Dumplings - Jamaica
    - Johnny Cake - Bahamian
    - Lemon Pudding - St. Croix
    - Mango Bread Pudding with Rum Sauce - Bahamas
    - Roti - Jamaica

10. Desserts & Cakes 192
    - Carrot Cake
    - Coconut Cake
    - Key Lime Pie
    - Lemon Cake
    - Peach Tart
    - Strawberry Cake

Glossary 204
Acknowledgements 216
About the Author 217

Chapter 1

Beverages & Cocktails

- Always Sunny Never Scurvy, Martini
- Bahamian Sky Juice
- Banana and Papaya Smoothie (Non-Alcoholic)
- Blue Moon over Miami Martini
- Coconut and Mango Smoothie (Non-Alcoholic)
- Cuba-Cranny
- Daiquiri (Mango, Banana, Pineapple, Peach, Frozen)
- Dark & Stormy
- Ginger Beer (Non-Alcoholic)
- Guava and Lime Juice (Non-Alcoholic)
- Hail Miami Mary
- Key Lime Margarita
- Key Lime Pie Cocktail
- Mojito
- Pina colada
- Planter's Punch
- Ponche de Crème (Trinidad's Christmas drink)
- Rum Punch
- Simple Syrup
- South Beach Sunrise
- Ting with a Sting
- Welcome to the Island Drink

Always Sunny Never Scurvy, Martini

A fresh tribute to one of my favorite cities. This classy twist of a tropical mimosa is homage to brunch by the pool at my favorite Miami Beach Hotel, the Fountain Blu. Enjoy!

In a cocktail shaker pour
    1/2 tsp. Lime juice
    4 oz. Champagne
    2 oz. Tangerine Vodka

Gently stir with ice then strain into a chilled martini glass.

Serve in chilled martini glass.
Garnish with an orange twist.

Serves: 1

Bahamian Sky Juice

4 ripe coconuts
1 cup evaporated milk
1 cup gin or rum
3 T sugar (optional)
1 tsp. ground cinnamon
½ tsp. freshly grated nutmeg

Use a screwdriver to poke the eye of the coconut and drain the liquid through a strainer into a mixing bowl. Add remaining ingredients and mix in a gallon jug.

Chill for two hours, or add ice cubes.

Serves: 4

Banana & Papaya Smoothie

(Non-Alcoholic)

3 large ripe bananas
1 large papaya
½ cup soy milk
1 ½ cup water
1 cup cubed ice
½ cup oats
3 tablespoons honey
½ teaspoon nutmeg

Soak oats in water for 5 minutes. Add all the ingredients to the blender. Blend until it reaches rich texture. Serve chilled for breakfast.

Serves: 2

Blue Moon over Miami Martini

In a cocktail shaker pour
    2 oz. Ouzo
    1 oz. blue Curaçao
    Splash of tonic water
    ½ cup ice

Shake until chilled. Strain into a chilled martini glass.

Garnish with an orange twist.

Serves: 1

Coconut & Mango Smoothie

2 large mangos, peeled and deseeded
½ cup coconut flesh
2 cup rich coconut milk
1 ½ cups ice
10 mint leaves
2 teaspoons natural cane sugar
2 teaspoons lime juice

Add first four ingredients to the blender. Blend until it reaches smooth and rich texture. Muddle sugar and mint together. Finish smoothie with mint sugar and fresh lime juice.

Serves: 2

Cuba-crany

4 fluid ounces Puerto Rican white rum
1/2 lemon, juiced
6 fluid ounces cranberry juice
4 cubes ice

Place 4 ice cubes in two 6-ounce glasses. Pour 2 ounces of Puerto Rican white rum in each glass. Squeeze the juice of 1/4 of lemon in each glass. Pour in 3 ounces of cranberry juice. Stir.

Serves: 2

Source: Allrecipes

Daiquiris

Mango, Peach, Pineapple, Banana, Frozen

Basic Daiquiri Recipe
  2 ounces light rum
  2 tablespoons lime juice
  1-teaspoon superfine sugar
  3-4 finely crushed ice cubes

Combine all the ingredients in a cocktail shaker, and shake vigorously. Strain into a thoroughly chilled 4-ounce cocktail glass. Garnish with a lime twist.
Serves: 1

Variations
Add these flavorful ingredients to the above basic recipe for a tropical delight. Always use the best fresh ingredients.

Mango Daiquiris
  1/2 ounce Curacao
  1/4 cup finely chopped fresh mango

Peach Daiquiri
  ½ medium-sized ripe fresh peach peeled and coarsely chopped.

Pineapple Daiquiri
  ½ ounce Cointreau
  ½ cup pineapple juice

Banana Daiquiri
  ½ ounce banana liqueur
  ½ ounce lime juice
  ½ small banana, peeled and coarsely chopped

Frozen Daiquiris
  Place all ingredients in an electric blender and blend at high speed until the contents have the consistency of snow. Pour into a thoroughly chilled 6-ounce glasses and serve with fruit and a tiny umbrella.

Serves: 1

Dark and Stormy

The origin of this cocktail came from Bermuda, where the Goslings ginger beer and dark rum rule the world. Once you try this drink you'll be hooked.

In a tall glass fill with ice and add
6 oz. Ginger beer

Float 1 oz. of Gosslings Black rum on top.

Serve with a lime wedge.

Serves: 1

Gay Island Christmas

3 oz. Coco Lopez, well stirred
6 oz. Baileys
6 oz. Pineapple juice
1 small banana, sliced
6 oz. red rum (Mount Gay, Cruzan, Vat 19,)
Garnish: nutmeg, maraschino cherry & sprig of mint

Fill blender with ice. Combine ingredients & blend until ice is crushed & mixture is smooth.

Serve immediately in cocktail glasses, topped with grated nutmeg & garnished with a maraschino cherry & sprig of mint.
Serves: 4

Source web: recipes.caribseek.com Chef Gerda Dehrmann

Ginger Beer

½ pound young ginger
¼ cup natural cane sugar
1 gallon water
2 tablespoon lemon juice

Grate ginger on fine setting or pulse in blender with water. Strain through fine strainer.
Use fresh cane juice if available. Alternate dilute ¼ cup cane sugar into ¼ cup water over low flame, cool before adding to ginger.

Serve over ice with minced ginger.

Guava & Lime Juice

(non-alcoholic)
12 fresh guava
3 limes
6 cups water
1 teaspoon young ginger
10 leaves fresh basil

Puree guava and fresh ginger with water for 30 seconds. Adjust water to right consistency; juice should have a smooth light texture.
Halve the limes and press with reamer to extract the juices. Add lime to guava juice and strain together through fine strainer.
Add torn basil leave with strained juice into pitcher; serve over ice.

Serves: 4

Hail Miami Mary

In a cocktail shaker pour
- 4 oz. tomato juice
- 2 oz. pepper vodka
- 2 oz. orange vodka
- 1/2 tsp. Worcester sauce
- 1/2 tsp. Prepared Horseradish
- 1/2 tsp. Lemon Juice
- 1/4 tsp. Celery salt
- 1/4 tsp. Old Bay Seasoning

Shake together tomato juice, vodkas, Worcester sauce, horseradish, lemon juice and seasonings.

Rim glass with lemon juice and roll in Old Bay Seasoning. Pour mixture over ice into prepared glasses. Garnish with Lemon wedge, Celery Stalk, Green Olives.

Serves: 1

Key Lime Margarita

3 T Key Lime juice
1 cup Tequila gold
5 T Cointreau
4-5 cups crushed ice
Margarita salt (optional)
Key Lime slides for garnish

Dip rim of Margarita glass in a little Key Lime juice, then dip in a plate of Margarita salt and allow a few seconds to dry. In the container of a blender, combine lime juice, tequila and Cointreau. Blend on low for a few seconds, then add the crushed ice and turn to high speed till frozen drink consistency. Pour into Margarita glasses and garnish with lime slice.

Serves: 4
Source: Joyce LAFray, Key Lime Cookin'.

Key Lime Pie Cocktail

1/2 lime, cut into wedges
4 fluid ounces vodka
1 1/2 fluid ounces frozen limeade, concentrate, thawed
1 teaspoon vanilla extract
2 twists lime zest, garnish

Place the lime wedges in the bottom of a mixing glass and muddle them well. Cover with ice, and pour in vodka, lime juice, and vanilla. Shake well, then strain into two stemmed cocktail glasses. Garnish each with a twist of lime.

Serves: 2
Source: Allrecipes

Mojito

1/2 teaspoon confectioners' sugar
1/2 lime, juiced
1 sprig fresh mint, crushed
1/2 cup crushed ice
2 fluid ounces white rum
4 fluid ounces carbonated water
1 sprig fresh mint, garnish

In a highball glass, stir together the confectioners' sugar and lime juice. Bruise the mint leaves and drop into glass. Fill glass with crushed ice and pour in rum. Pour in carbonated water to fill the glass. Garnish with a sprig of mint.

Serves: 1

Pina Colada

4 oz. pineapple juice
2 oz. coconut cream
2 oz. golden rum
½ cup crushed ice
Pineapple stick
Maraschino cherry

Place all ingredients except pineapple stick and cherry into a blender blend until slushy. Pour unstrained into a highball glass.

Garnish with pineapple and cherry.

Serves: 1

Planter's Punch

2 tablespoons fresh lime juice
2 teaspoons simple syrup
3 oz. dark Jamaican rum
Dash of Angostura bitters
½ cup finely crushed ice
Maraschino cherry

Combine the lime juice, syrup, rum, bitters, and crushed ice in a cocktail shaker and shake vigorously. Pour, unstrained, into a small tumbler. Decorate with the cherry.

Serves: 1

Rum Punch – Antiqua

1 oz lime juice
1 oz pineapple juice
1 oz orange juice
1 oz grenadine
2 oz light rum
3-4 ice cubes
Nutmeg

Combine the juices, grenadine, ice cubes and rum in a cocktail shaker and shake vigorously. Strain into a small tumbler and grate a little nutmeg on top.

Serves: 1

Ponche de Crème

(Trinidad's Christmas drink)

6 eggs
2 oz. of lime juice
4 cups of evaporated milk
1 1/2 cups of sweetened condensed milk
3/4 cup dark spiced rum
2 tsp. bitters
¼ tsp. grated nutmeg

Beat together six eggs with 2 oz. of lime juice.
Add 4 cups of evaporated milk and 1 1/2 cups of sweetened condensed milk and beat for another 30 seconds.
Add 3/4 cup dark spiced rum, 2 tsp. bitters and 1/4 tsp. grated nutmeg and beat for another minute. Chill before serving.

Serves: 4

Simple Syrup

Sugar does not dissolve readily with alcohol; for this reason superfine sugar is best in drinks. Simple syrup gives a much smoother syrup and is very easy to make.

2 cups granulated sugar
2 cups cold water

Combine sugar and water in a bowl. Stir from time to time until sugar is dissolved. Use in drinks instead of sugar.

½ ounce (1 tablespoon) equals 1 ½ teaspoons sugar.

South Beach Sunrise

2 oz. Bacardi Pineapple rum
1 oz. Bacardi Black rum
1 oz. Bacardi Coconut Rum
2 oz. Tonic tater
Splash of Orange juice

In a tall glass fill with ice, pour in all ingredients and top with a splash of orange juice.

Garnish with slice of orange, cherry and umbrella.
Serves: 1

Ting with a Sting

1 oz. rum
5 oz. Ting

Add 1 oz. rum to 5 oz. of Ting, a local grapefruit flavored soda. Serve over ice.
Serves: 1

Welcome to the Island Drink

2 oz. Bacardi Pineapple rum
2 oz. Bacardi Coconut rum
2 oz. Bacardi Silver rum
2 oz. Tonic water
Splash of orange juice
Nostrum flower

Pour over ice in a chilled cocktail shaker. Stir then serve over ice in a tall hurricane glass. Garnish with a nostrum flower inside the glass. Welcome to the Island.

Serves: 1

Chapter 2

Appetizers

- Akkra Bean Fritters
- Artichoke Leek Frittata
- Cassava chips
- Coconut Roasted Bananas
- Empanadas
- Fritters
- Ginger Beer Roasted Pineapple
- Mofongo plantain spread
- Phulouri split pea fritters
- Picklises
- Platanutri plantain chips
- Sweet potato chips
- Tostones de Platano, green plantain chips

Akkra Bean Fritters

1 cup black-eyed peas, or soy beans
2 fresh hot peppers, seeded and chopped
2 teaspoons of salt
Oil for frying

Soak the beans overnight in cold water. Drain, rub off and discard the skin, cover beans again with cold water and soak for 2 or 3 hours longer. Drain, rinse, and put in food processor. Grind the peppers. Add the salt and peppers to the beans and beat with a wooden spoon until they are light and fluffy and considerable increased in bulk.

Heat oil in a heavy frying pan and fry the mixture by tablespoonful until golden brown on both sides. Drain on paper towels. Serve hot as an accompaniment to drinks.

Prep time: 20 minutes
Cook time: 35 minutes
Yield: 24 fritters

Source: The Complete Book of Caribbean Cooking

Artichoke Leek Frittata

2 Tbsp butter
2 cups sliced, cleaned leeks, white and green parts only (sliced in half lengthwise, then sliced crosswise, about ¼-inch thick slices)
4 ounces frozen artichoke hearts, thawed, sliced into 1/2 – inch slices
½ teaspoon dried tarragon (can sub 2 teaspoons of chopped fresh tarragon, or dried herbes de provence or dried thyme)
¼ teaspoon Kosher salt
5 eggs
8 ounces (1 cup) small curd cottage cheese (can use ricotta if you prefer)
2 Tbsp all purpose flour (omit for gluten-free version)
½ teaspoon baking powder
1 cup grated Parmesan cheese
Fresh chopped chives or parsley for garnish

In an 8 to 9 inch ovenproof stick-free pan or well-seasoned cast iron pan, melt butter on medium heat. Add the sliced leeks and gently cook until softened, about 10 minutes. Add the artichoke hearts, tarragon, and salt. Cook until the artichoke hearts are warmed through, then remove from pan to a bowl and set aside.

In a medium bowl, whisk together the eggs and the cottage cheese. In a small bowl, whisk together the eggs and cottage cheese. In a small bowl, whisk together the flour, Parmesan, and baking powder. Add the flour mixture to the egg mixture and whisk. Stir the artichokes and leeks into the egg mixture.

Wipe out the pan with a paper towel. Then melt another tablespoon of butter into the pan on medium heat, and swirl along the bottom and sides to coat well. Pour the egg mixture in to the pan, swirling to make sure the artichokes and leeks are evenly distributed. Lower the heat. Cover the pan; slowly cook on the stovetop for 12 to 15 minutes, until all but the center has set.

Place rack in upper third of oven. Preheat the broiler. When the frittata is mostly set, except for the center which is still wiggly, place the pan in the oven. Broil for 3 to 4 minutes until the top is lightly browned and the center has set.

Remove pan from the oven. Use a blunt knife or metal spatula to loosen the edges of the frittata from the pan. Gently insert the spatula under the frittata to loosen it from the bottom of the pan. Then gently slide the frittata onto a serving plate.

Garnish with chives or parsley to serve.

Prep time: 20 minutes
Cook time: 35 minutes
Serves: 4

Source: Simply Recipes

Cassava Chips

Cassava root
Oil for deep frying
Salt

Peel the cassava root and slice, crosswise, as thinly as possible. Steep in iced water for 30 minutes, drain and dry on paper towels.

Fry until delicately browned and crisp in deep oil heated to 370° on a frying thermometer. Drain on paper towels, sprinkle with salt, and serve as an accompaniment to drinks.

Prep time: 5 minutes
Cook time: 15 minutes
Yield: 24 fritters

Source: The Complete Book of Caribbean Cooking

Coconut Roasted Bananas

6 Bananas
1/3 Cup dark brown sugar
½ cup coconut milk
¼ teaspoon grated nutmeg

Preheat oven to 375°F.
Peel bananas and place in 9x9 baking dish. Pour coconut milk over the bananas. Sprinkle with sugar and grate the nutmeg on top of the bananas. Roast the bananas until they are slightly brown on top. Serve warm.

Prep time: 5 minutes
Cook time: 15 minutes
Yield: Serves 6

Source: Sips, Bites & Sweets, Ras Rody Organics

Empanadas

Traditionally made with meat filling this version is yummy and simple.

1 cup masa harina P.A.N., or pre-cooked corn meal*
1 cup boiling water
1 teaspoon salt
1 teaspoon salt
1 teaspoon sugar
1 cup all purpose flour
2 eggs (save one for later)
2 tablespoons sweet butter, melted and cooled
1/3 cup grated Edam or Gouda cheese

Put the corn meal into a basin. Stir in the boiling water. Cool. Add the salt, sugar, flour and egg, mix and turn out onto a floured board. Knead until smooth. Return to the bowl and add the melted butter, grated cheese, mixing well.

Roll out onto a lightly floured board. Cut into circles about 4-inches in diameter. Put 1 tablespoon of filling on each circle and fold over into a half-moon shape. Brush the edges with beaten egg and seal well. Turn the edges over to the top side to make a quadruple thickness and pinch into scallops with the fingers. Fry in deep hot oil until golden brown (370' on a frying thermometer).

Serve hot as first course, or as an accompaniment to drinks.

Filling:
2 tablespoons unsalted butter
½ pound tofu crumbles
1 tablespoon finely chopped onion
1 tablespoon finely chopped celery
2 tablespoons seeded and chopped bell pepper
1 medium tomato, peeled, seeded and chopped
Salt
Fresh ground pepper

Heat the butter in a frying pan an sauté the tofu crumbles, onion, celery and bell pepper until done, about 15 minutes. Add the tomato, salt, freshly ground pepper. Cook 3 to 4 minutes longer. Cool. Use to stuff the empanadas.

*Note: the corn meal used for the empanadas is similar to the corn meal used for Mexican tortillas. Dried Corn is soaked, boiled, ground and dried. However, the Venezuelan corn as a very different flavor from Mexican corn, and it is not possible to substitute Mexican masa harina. Several packaged brands are available in Latin American groceries.

Prep time: 20 minutes
Cook time: 35 minutes
Yield: 20 empanadas
Source: The Complete Book of Caribbean Cooking

Fritters

1 cup all-purpose flour
1 ½ teaspoons baking powder
1 teaspoon salt
4 eggs
4 ounces dried seaweed
4 shallots chopped
½ cup chopped fresh parsley
1 small hot pepper
2 teaspoons unsalted butter, melted and cooled
2 teaspoons vegetable oil
2 teaspoons rum

Sift the flour with the baking powder and salt into a bowl. Make a well in the center and add the eggs, butter, oil, and rum. Beat thoroughly until the batter is smooth. Let the batter stand 1 to 2 hours before using.

To make the fritters, mix the batter with 4 ounces dried seaweed.

For sweet fritters, add a tablespoon of sugar and add ¼ pound mashed or sliced bananas, or any suitable fruit.

Heat vegetable oil in deep kettle. Drop fritter mixture by tablespoonsful into the hot oil. Fry until golden brown on both sides. Drain on paper towels.

Prep time: 2 hours
Cook time: 30 minutes
Yield: 24 fritters
Source: The Complete Book of Caribbean Cooking

Ginger Beer Roasted Pineapple

1 ripe pineapple
24 oz. ginger beer
1 bay laurel leaf

Cook the ginger beer with the bay leaf over medium high heat until it becomes syrup.

Preheat oven to 375°F.

Clean and peel the pineapple, cut into ½ inch cubes.

Toss the chunks in enough syrup to lightly coat them.
Reserve some syrup for sauce.
Place pineapple in a large baking pan

Roast at 375°F until slightly brown.

Prep time: 20 hours
Cook time: 20 minutes
Yield: 20 chunks
Source: The Complete Book of Caribbean Cooking

Monfongo Plantain Spread

4 half ripe plantains
oil for frying
4 cloves crushed garlic
salt to taste

Peel the plantains and cut into 1-inch slices. Heat oil in the 10-12 inch frying pan. Fry as many at time as will fit, until golden brown on both sides.

Drain on paper towels and grind the cooked plantains in a mortar with the garlic until creamy. Season to taste with salt and serve spread on bread or crackers, or make into small balls. Serve as an appetizer with drinks.

It is important that the plantains be midway between green and ripe. Green, they will have the sticky consistency they have in foo-foo, ripe they will be too sweet.

Prep time: 30 minutes
Cook time: 30 minutes
Yield: 24 fritters
Source: The Complete Book of Caribbean Cooking

Phulouri Split Pea Fritters

1 cup split peas
1 medium onion, chopped
1 clove garlic, chopped
Salt
Pepper
Oil for deep-frying

Soak the split peas overnight in cold water to cover. Drain thoroughly. Put through the fine blade of a food mill with the onion and garlic, or reduce to a puree in an electric blender. Season highly with salt and pepper and beat with a wooden spoon until light and fluffy or use an electric beater.

Heat the oil in a frying pan. Form the mixture, a tablespoonful at a time, into balls and drop into the hot oil, about 6 at a time. Fry until brown all over. Drain on paper towels. Serve hot, each stuck with a toothpick, as an appetizer.

If liked, a tablespoon of curry powder may be added to the split peas when they are ground. A hot pepper sauce is often served as a dip for the Phulouri.

Prep time: 2 hours
Cook time: 30 minutes
Yield: 24 fritters
Source: The Complete Book of Caribbean Cooking

Picklises

Green beans, cut French-style
Cabbage, very finely shredded
Cauliflower, separated into flowerets
Carrots, scraped and thinly sliced
Onion, thinly sliced
Tender young green peas
Radishes, thinly sliced
3 fresh hot red peppers pricked in 2 or 3 places with a fork
Vinegar

Prepare equal amounts of the vegetables and place in a large crock or jar. Cover with vinegar and allow standing in a cool place for 1 week. Serve as relish with crackers and cheese as an accompaniment to drinks. Store in the refrigerator.

Prep time: 2 hours
Cook time: 30 minutes
Yield: 24 fritters
Source: The Complete Book of Caribbean Cooking

Plantanutri Plantain Chips

Green or half ripe plantains
Salt
Oil for frying

Peel the plantains, and slice crosswise as thickly as possible. Drop into salted ice water and let stand for 30 minutes. Drain, and dry on paper towels. Fry until delicately browned in deep oil heated to 370°. Drain on paper towels, sprinkle with salt and serve as an accompaniment to drinks. In St. Kitts green bananas are cooked in this way. The result is very delicate.

Prep time: 2 hours
Cook time: 30 minutes
Yield: 24 fritters
Source: The Complete Book of Caribbean Cooking

Sweet Potato Chips

1 pound white (boniato) sweet potatoes
oil for frying
Salt

Wash and peel the sweet potatoes and slice as thinly as possible. Soak for 1 hour in cold, salted water. Drain and dry on paper towels. Fry until delicately browned in deep oil. Drain on paper towels, sprinkle with salt. Keep warm in oven until ready to serve, or serve at room temperature, as an accompaniment to drinks. Serve with a dip.

Prep time: 2 hours
Cook time: 30 minutes
Yield: Serves 4 or more.
Source: The Complete Book of Caribbean Cooking

Tostones Puerto Rican Fried Plantains

5 tablespoons vegetable oil
1 green plantain
3 cups cold water
Salt to taste

Heat the oil in a large skillet. Place the plantains in the oil and fry on both sides; approximately 3 1/2 minutes per side. Remove the plantains from the pan and flatten the plantains by placing a plate over the fried plantains and pressing down. Dip the plantains in water, then return them to the hot oil and fry 1 minute on each side. Salt to taste and serve immediately.

Crispy fried plantains. A plantain is a very firm banana.

Serves: 4
Prep: Time: approx. 15 Minutes
Cook: Time: approx. 30 Minutes
Source: Tony from Puerto Rico

Chapter 3

Soups & Stews

- Black Bean Soup - Trini Style
- Callaloo Soup
- Chili, Jamaican Me Crazy - Jamaica
- Corn Soup - Trini Style
- Groundnut Soup – St. Kitts
- Lentil Soup
- Mushroom Barley Soup
- Okra & Tomato Stew
- Pepperpot Apple's Antiqua
- Pepperpot Jamaican Soup
- Pepperpot Antiquan
- Picadillo Crockpot
- Pumpkin Soup - Jamaica
- Red Pea Stew with dumplings – St. Croix
- Veggie Burger Chowder - Bermuda

Black Bean Soup, Trini Sytle

1 pound black beans (2 cups dry or 2 cans)
1 medium onion
2 cloves garlic, crushed
2 sprigs parsley
1 sprig thyme, or ½ teaspoon dried
2 small stalks celery with leaves, chopped
4 scallions, chopped, using white and green parts
Bay leaf
6 cups vegetable stock
Fresh ground pepper
Salt
Pepper wine

If using dry beans, soak the beans overnight in cold water. Drain, and discard water.

Put the beans into a large saucepan or soup kettle. Add the onion, garlic, parsley, thyme, celery, scallions, bay leaf, vegetable stock, and pepper.

Bring to a boil, lower the heat, cover and simmer until the beans are very tender, about 2 hours. Discard bay leaf.

Puree the soup in an electric blender, or with an immersion blender. Add salt if needed.

Add a little pepper wine to each serving.

Serves: 8
Prep Time: approx. 1 hour
Cook Time: approx. 2 hours
Source: Keevin from Trini

Callaloo Soup

1 pound callaloo leaves or spinach
6 cups veggie stock
1 onion, chopped
1/2 pound salt tofu crumbles
6 tablespoons minced shallots
1/4 teaspoon dried thyme
1 green chili pepper, chopped
1 cup okra
1/2 pound tempeh

Remove the thick stems of the callaloo leaves, chop roughly, and put into a large saucepan. Add the stock, onion, tofu crumbles, black pepper, shallots, thyme, chili pepper, and tempeh. Cover, and simmer until tender, about 35 minutes.

Add the okra, and cook for 8 minutes. Remove the chili pepper. Puree the soup in a blender or food processor. Reheat, and adjust seasonings.

A taste of the Caribbean. The main ingredients are callaloo leaves, or spinach, and okra. Both were originally brought from Africa in the seventeenth century. Serve piping hot with slices of avocado and hot bread.

Serves: 6
Prep Time: approx. 15 Minutes
Cook Time: approx. 30 Minutes
Adapted from Source: Allrecipes

Chili, Jamaican Me Crazy - Jamaica

1 1/2 pounds tofu crumbles
1 teaspoon olive oil
1 1/2 cups chopped onion
2 cloves garlic, crushed
2 1/2 cups chopped yellow bell pepper
1 tablespoon ground cumin
1 tablespoon hot paprika
1 tablespoon chili powder
2 teaspoons white sugar
1/2 teaspoon salt
1/4 teaspoon ground cloves
2 (14.5 ounce) cans stewed tomatoes
1 (15 ounce) can kidney beans, drained
1 (15 ounce) can black beans, drained
1 (15 ounce) can cannellini beans
1 (6 ounce) can tomato paste
2 tablespoons balsamic vinegar
1/3 cup chopped fresh cilantro

Coat a large Dutch oven with cooking spray and place over medium-high heat. When pan is hot add the olive oil and sauté the onion and garlic until the onion is tender, then put in the yellow pepper and cook until tender.

Season with cumin, paprika, chili powder, sugar, salt and cloves. Stir in the stewed tomatoes, kidney beans, black beans and cannellini beans.

Add water to cover and simmer for 30 minutes. Remove from heat, stir in the vinegar and serve hot topped with fresh cilantro. Serve this dish by itself or over a bowl of basmati rice.

Serves: 12
Prep Time: approx. 15 Minutes
Cook Time: approx. 30 Minutes

Corn Soup, Trini Style

1 cup split peas
1 cup channa (garbanzo), soaked overnight
6 – 8 cups water
1 onion
3 cloves garlic
1 chive stalk
1 celery stalk
2 pimento peppers
4 ears of corn
1 carrot
1 cup pumpkin
1 pk vegetable soup
For dumpling:
1/4 cup flour
1/4 cup cornmeal
water

Wash the channa and pressure-cook for about 15 minutes. Pressure-cook the split peas for about 10 minutes. Knead the dough for the cornmeal dumpling to a semi-stiff dough, and cut into 1/2" pieces. Set aside.

Clean and chop the corn into 1 -2" pieces (notice the technique; just press down the point of the knife into the corn). Chop up the rest of ingredients (carrots, pimento, chive, celery, pumpkin) and add to pot of water.

When boiling, add corn, dumplings, split peas and channa and allow simmering for about 20 mins or until the corn is cooked and the dumplings float to the surface. Stir occasionally.

Serves: 8
Prep Time: approx. 30 Minutes
Cook Time: approx. 30 Minutes
Source: Keevin from Trini

Groundnut Soup

Peanuts are often called groundnuts in the English-speaking islands.

4 ounces (¾ cup) peeled and roasted peanuts
5 cups vegetable stock
Salt
Fresh ground pepper
Pickapper hot pepper sauce, or Tabasco
1 cup heavy cream or evaporated milk or Almond Milk
1 tablespoon Angostura bitters
Dry sherry, or dry vermouth (optional)
Croutons
Chopped chives

Put the peanuts and stock to cover in an electric blender and blend on high speed to a smooth paste. Pour into a heavy saucepan; add the rest of the stock, season to taste with salt and pepper and hot sauce. Cook over low heat, stir in the heavy cream and cook, stirring, until heated through. Stir in the Angostura bitters.

A tablespoon of dry sherry, or dry vermouth, may be added to each serving. Garnish with croutons and serve hot. Or chill and serve with chives.

Serves: 6
Prep Time: approx. 30 Minutes.
Cook Time: approx. 30 Minutes.
Source: The Complete guide to Caribbean Cooking

Lentil Soup

1 cup green lentils
7 cups water
2 carrots
½ bulb of celery root
3 cloves garlic
3 sprigs fresh oregano
¼ teaspoon scotch bonnet pepper
1 teaspoon coconut oil or other vegetable oil

Roast garlic for 1 hour. Place in aluminum foil with coconut oil; roast at 275° oven until soft and develops strong fragrance.

Bring the coconut milk and water to boil in large pot. Cut the carrot and celery root into ½ inch dice.

Add to boiling pot with lentils and roasted garlic.

Bring to boil again and then reduce heat and simmer for up to three hours over low heat.

Add picked oregano and minced scotch bonnet pepper just before serving.

Serve with sweet festival bread.

Serves: 8
Prep Time: approx. 15 Minutes
Cook Time: approx. 60 Minutes
Adapted from Source: Ras Rody Organics

Mushroom & Barley Soup

3 cups sliced baby bella mushrooms
2 cups mushroom medley
1 cup 10 Min. Barley (Trader Joes)
1 quart vegetable stock
3/4 cup Masala Wine
1 small diced onion
2 celery stocks, diced
2 carrot sticks, sliced
2 garlic cloves, minced
2 tablespoon shallots, minced
¼ cup soy creamer
5 whole bay leaves
1 teaspoon thyme
1 teaspoon rosemary
1 tablespoon cumin
1 teaspoon salt
1 teaspoon pepper
1 teaspoon Old Bay seasoning
1 bunch parsley, finely copped

Clean and slice mushrooms and veggies and herbs (except parsley). Place in large stockpot.

Sauté till mushrooms are soft. Add 1-quart vegetable stock, cumin, and old bay. Then add the 10 Min Barley, ¼ cup soy creamer, and the chopped parsley. Salt and Pepper to taste.

Simmer for 30 min. Serve warm.

Serves: 8
Prep Time: approx. 15 Minutes
Cook Time: approx. 30 Minutes
Source: Pam Merkle

Okra & Tomato Stew

1 tablespoon vegetable oil
1 clove garlic, minced
1 medium onion, finely chopped
1 medium green bell pepper, finely chopped
1/2 (16 ounce) package frozen okra, thawed and sliced
8 ounces fresh mushrooms, sliced
1 (6 ounce) can tomato paste
1 (14.5 ounce) can diced tomatoes with juice
1/2 teaspoon file powder*
2 bay leaves
1 teaspoon salt
1 teaspoon ground black pepper
2 tablespoons vegetable oil
2 tablespoons all-purpose flour

Heat 1-tablespoon oil in a large saucepan over medium heat. Stir in garlic, onion, and green bell pepper, and sauté until tender. Stir in okra, mushrooms, diced tomatoes and their liquid, tomato paste, file powder, bay leaves, salt, and pepper. Cook, stirring occasionally, 40 minutes.

Heat 2 tablespoons oil in a medium skillet over medium heat. Stirring constantly, add flour, and cook 2 to 5 minutes, until a golden brown roux has formed. Spoon the roux into the okra mixture, and continue to cook, stirring occasionally, 5 to 10 minutes, until thickened.

*File powder is a seasoning made from the ground, dried leaves of the sassafras tree. It's an integral part of Creole cooking, and is used to thicken and flavor Gumbos and other Creole dishes.

Serves: 8
Prep Time: approx. 15 Minutes
Cook Time: approx. 40 Minutes
Adapted from Source: Karen Garnett.

Pepperpot Apples - Antiqua

This recipe is presented in the original vernacular of the author, Apple. Feel free to adjust ingredients and measurements to your personal taste.

1 apple
4 popa
6 anchoba
1 squach
10 ochra
1 bunch spanish
Salt
Pumpkin
Onion
Season pepper
Sweetpepper
Tofu

Get all the vegetable in a pot, put then to boil, when they are half finish cook, through in your pickle "swine" as the rastaman would say.

Let it continue to boil until the veg. Start to lint way, put in your seasons which is what I gave to you, at that time you should finish mixed your dumpling, so you put in your dumpling, keep sterling add a little cooking butter to give it a taste.

Taste it to make sure it taste nice, then you mixed a littler flour in some water and through it in to get it a little thick, and you are finish.

Serve as usual. Take it from me. "nuf respect" "apple"

Serves: 8
Prep time: approx. 15 minutes
Cook time: approx. 30 minutes
Source: www.caribbeanads.com

Pepperpot - Antiguan

10oz frozen spinach
1 medium eggplant (cut into small pieces)
1 small green squash (peeled, cut into small pieces)
2 medium zucchinis (cut into small pieces)
1 tsp. flour (for thickening)
2 salted tempeh (soaked over night, cut into small pieces)
1lb. of Jackfruit
5 okra pods
Salt, black pepper, 4 cloves garlic to taste
Optional- you use canned peas add at end or frozen pigeon peas or lima beans.

For dumplings:
1/2 lb. flour
1/4 cup of cornmeal

Cut all vegetables into small pieces put into pot with beans, cover with water. Once the pot starts boiling mix flour and corn meal together for dumplings and put into pot; taste test add salt, pepper etc.

Add dumplings let cook for about 1 1/2 hours; Watch your pot, don't let it burn, let vegetables and beans cook.

Add okras when almost finished cooking. To thicken the pepperpot if it is too thin, add flour to water and mix, then stir into the pepperpot.

Pepperpot takes about 2 1/2 hours to 3 hours to cook down to a smooth consistency.

Serves: 8 - 12
Prep Time: approx. 20 Minutes
Cook Time: approx. 2 Hours 40 Minutes
Source: www.caribbeanads.com

Pepperpot – Jamaican Soup

1 pound tempeh
1 pound beans (use what you have)
1/2 cup chopped onion
1/2 cup chopped celery
3 leeks, chopped
1 bunch fresh parsley, chopped
2 green bell peppers, diced
2 quarts vegetable stock
1/4 teaspoon dried thyme
1/2 teaspoon dried marjoram
1/2 teaspoon ground cloves (optional)
1/4 teaspoon crushed red pepper flakes
1 bay leaf
1 teaspoon ground black pepper
1 large potato, peeled and diced
2 large carrots, diced
4 tablespoons margarine or butter
4 tablespoons all-purpose flour

Cut the tempeh into 1/4-inch pieces. Place the tempeh in a large heavy kettle, sauté the tempeh. Add the onion, celery, leeks, parsley, and green peppers; sauté until tender. Stir in the bean, stock, thyme, marjoram, cloves, red pepper flakes, bay leaf, and black pepper. Bring the kettle to a boil, and turn down to a simmer. Cook, covered, until beans are very tender, about 2 hours. Add the diced potato and carrots, and cook for an additional 20 minutes.

Prepare the roux by stirring the flour into the melted butter or margarine, and cooking for a moment on the stove. When the soup is done to your liking, stir in the roux. Simmer, stirring all the while, until the soup thickens a bit.

Serves: 8 - 12
Prep Time: approx. 20 Minutes
Cook Time: approx. 2 Hours 40 Minutes
Source: DL Phelps

Picadillo CrockPot

1 pound ground Tofu crumbles
2 large onions, chopped
2 cloves garlic, chopped
1 tablespoon raisins
1 green capsicum pepper, chopped
1 red capsicum pepper, chopped
1 teaspoon chili powder
1 teaspoon salt
1 teaspoon dried oregano
1/2 teaspoon ground cumin
1/2 teaspoon pepper
2 cloves garlic finely chopped
1 10 ounce cans diced tomatoes
1 10 ounce can green chilies undrained
1/2 cup slivered almonds toasted
Olives, capers, peppers to garnish

Cook onion in 12 inch skillet over medium heat, stirring occasionally until onions are brown; stir in the tofu crumbles.

Mix Tofu crumbles mixture and remaining ingredients except almonds in 3 1/2 to 6 quart slow cooker. Cover and cook on low heat setting 3 hours or until most of the liquid is absorbed. Stir in almonds.

Picadillo is traditionally served topped with a fried egg and fried plantains, and with black beans and rice.

Serves: 6
Prep Time: approx. 15 minutes
Cook Time: approx. 3 hours
Adapted from Source: www.geocities.com/webcipes2

Pumpkin Soup - Jamaican

1 fresh pumpkin
2 cups unsweetened pumpkin puree
2 cups coconut milk
5 cups water
2 potatoes, peeled
2 sprigs fresh thyme
6 leaves fresh sage
1 stick cinnamon bark
2 tablespoons olive oil
1 teaspoon black pepper

Cut the pumpkin in half, deseed and rub with coconut oil.

Place the thyme sprigs and sage on both halves and wrap in aluminum foil.

Place over open flame or in 350°F oven and roast until flesh is tender. Scoop flesh from peel. Bring coconut milk and water to boil in large pot. Add pumpkin and chopped potato to pot.

Let it simmer for 3 hours with one stick of cinnamon bark and fresh sage leaves. Puree in blender until smooth, finish with fresh olive oil and black pepper.

Serve in calabash bowls with roasted almonds.

Serves: 6
Prep Time: approx. 15 minutes
Cook Time: approx. 3 hours
Adapted from Source: Ras Rody Organics

Red Pea Stew – Jamaica

2 cups red peas
2 cups coconut milk
2 cups water
2 potatoes
2 carrots
8 okra
2 tablespoons fresh ginger
3 sprigs fresh thyme
½ teaspoon allspice

Soak the red peas overnight. Cook the peas with coconut milk and water for 30 minutes.

Dice the potatoes, carrots, and okra into ¼ inch cubes while the peas are cooking.

Add diced vegetables and cook on low heat until stew is rick and creamy.

Season with grated fresh ginger and allspice.

Finish with picked thyme and serve warm over brown rice.

Serves: 6
Prep Time: approx. 15 minutes
Cook Time: approx. 3 hours
Adapted from Source: Ras Rody Organics

Veggie Burger Chowder - Bermuda

2 tablespoons vegetable oil
3 stalks celery, chopped
2 carrots, chopped
1 onion, chopped
1 green bell pepper, chopped
3 cloves garlic, minced
3 tablespoons tomato paste
4 cups veggie stock
2 potatoes, peeled and cubed
1 (14.5 ounce) can peeled and diced tomatoes
2 tablespoons Worcestershire sauce
1 jalapeno pepper, seeded and minced
1 teaspoon ground black pepper
1 bay leaf
1 pound veggie burgers, cut into 1 inch pieces

Heat oil in a large soup pot over medium heat. Add celery, carrots, onion, green pepper, and garlic; sauté about 8 minutes. Stir in tomato paste, and cook 1 minute.

Add veggie stock, potatoes, canned tomatoes with juice, Worcestershire sauce, jalapeno pepper, bay leaf, and ground black pepper. Simmer until potatoes are tender, stirring about every 30 minutes. Add veggie burger. Simmer about 10 minutes.

This recipe comes from the beautiful island of Bermuda. A wonderful blend of veggies and spices creates a meal in itself! Serve with a loaf of warm, crusty bread and Sherry Pepper Sauce to sprinkle on top.

Serves: 4-6
Prep Time: approx. 15 Minutes
Cook Time: approx. 30 Minutes
Source: Allrecipes

Chapter 4

Sauces

- Coconut and Sage Carmel Sauce - Jamaica
- Coconut Sauce - Jamaica
- Creole Sauce - Trinidad
- Habanero Lime Butter Sauce - Jamaica
- Jerk Rub - Jamaica
- Mango Chutney - - Jamaica
- Mango Jam - Jamaica
- Pepper Wine - Jamaica
- Pickled Scotch Bonnet Peppers / Homemade Pickapep - Jamaica
- Pineapple Jam - Jamaica
- Pineapple Sauce – Jamaica
- Salsa Rojo para Frijoles Negros, *Sweet Pepper Sauce for Black Beans* - Cuba
- Sauce Vinaigrette, *French Dressing* – French Islands
- Sofrito - Cuba

Coconut & Sage Carmel Sauce - Jamaica

½ cup coconut milk
½ cup coconut paste*
5 leaves fresh sage
½ cup brown sugar

In a saucepan heat sugar, on medium bring to a boil then simmer till it begins to caramelize. Do not stir the sugar as it cooks, for this will cause it to crystalize.

Once the sugar reaches a rich golden color, add the coconut milk and paste.

Stir together with wooden spoon until mixture is smooth and coats the back of the spoon. Remove from heat and steep with fresh sage.

Serve warm over warm carrot cake or Coconut and Sweet Potato Pudding.

*To make the paste, work tender coconut flesh in mortar and pestle until smooth, if you cannot make the paste, you can substitute an equal amount of coconut milk and cook the mixture a little longer.

Serves: 2-4
Prep Time: approx. 10 Minutes
Cook Time: approx. 20 Minutes
Source: Ras Rody Organics

Coconut Sauce - Jamaica

1 cup coconut milk
½ cup dark brown sugar
¼ cup raisins
Nutmeg

Roughly chop raisins.

In a heavy saucepan cook the coconut milk and sugar until the sugar dissolves and the sauce is thick enough to coat the back of the spoon, remove from heat.

Add the raisins and a touch of freshly grated nutmeg.

Serve warm as a drizzle on desserts.

Serves 2
Prep Time: approx. 5 Minutes
Cook Time: approx. 10 Minutes
Source: Ras Rody Organics

Creole Sauce - Trinidad

3 tablespoons vegetable oil
1 medium onion, finely chopped
1 green bell pepper, seeded and chopped
3 tablespoons all purpose flour
2 medium tomatoes, peeled and chopped
1 cup vegetable stock or dry white wine
Salt
Fresh ground pepper
1 teaspoon lime juice
1 teaspoon vinegar
Hot Pepper sauce to taste

Heat oil in a saucepan, add the onion and pepper, and sauté' until the onion is tender but not browned. Stir in the flour and cook, stirring constantly with a wooden spoon, for a minute or two until the flour is lightly browned. Add the tomatoes and stir to mix well.

Gradually stir in the stock or wine, season to taste with salt and pepper and cook, stirring until the sauce has thickened. Add the lime juice and vinegar, and hot pepper sauce to taste.

Yield 2 cups
Prep Time: approx. 15 Minutes
Cook Time: approx. 10 Minutes
Source: The Complete Book of Caribbean Cooking

Habanero Lime Butter - Jamaica

1/4-cup butter
1-tablespoon lime juice
2 teaspoons minced habanero pepper
2 teaspoons grated lime zest
1/4-teaspoon garlic salt

In a mixing bowl, using an electric mixer beat the butter until smooth. Mix in lime juice, habanero, lime zest, and garlic salt. Cover and refrigerate.

Prep Time: approx. 10 Minutes.

Jerk Rub - Jamaica

1 onion, finely chopped
½ cup finely chopped scallions
2 teaspoons fresh thyme leaves
2 teaspoons salt
1 teaspoon ground Jamaican pimento (all spice)
¼ teaspoon ground nutmeg
½ teaspoon ground cinnamon
4 to 6 hot peppers, finely ground
1 teaspoon ground black pepper

Mix together all the ingredients to make a paste. A food processor fitted with a steel blade is ideal for this. Store leftovers in the refrigerator in a tightly closed jar for about a month. Makes 1 cup.

Pastes made of spices, herbs, and onions are the authentic jerk flavoring method. Rub the paste into the uncooked Beans to add flavor. This is a medium-hot paste; it can be made hotter with the addition of more hot peppers or hot pepper sauce. If you want less heat, remove the seeds and membranes containing the seeds from the peppers before grinding them. Scotch bonnet or habanero peppers are preferred, but you can substitute the milder, more readily available jalapeño or Serrano peppers.

Prep Time: approx. 10 Minutes
Source: Web: Helen Willinsky

Mango Chutney - Jamaica

3 pounds hard, green (unripe) mangos, preferably a fleshy type
2 tablespoons salt
½ pound ripe tamarinds
2 cups vinegar, preferably Pickapepper cane vinegar, otherwise malt vinegar
3 cups West Indian brown sugar, or any light brown sugar
½ cup peeled and chopped fresh ginger root
½ cup seedless raisins
1 teaspoon ground allspice
1 ounce hot dried red peppers, seeded and roughly crumbled.

Peel the mangoes and cut the flesh off the seeds into pieces about 1-by-2 inches. Mix with the salt and set aside fro 2 hours. Pick the shell off the tamarinds, or use tamarind pulp, if available.

Cover with ½ cup boiling water; allow standing for about half an hour then forcing the pulp through a sieve. Discard the seeds. Drain the mangos thoroughly, discard the liquid and put into a large, heavy saucepan with the other ingredients and simmer, stirring from time to time, until the mixture is thick and the mangoes are tender, about half an hour. The mango pieces should not disintegrate. Pour into sterilized jars.

Yield: 3 1-pint jars
Prep Time: approx. 45 Minutes
Cook Time: approx. 30 Minutes
Adapted from source: The Complete Book of Caribbean Cooking

Mango Jam - Jamaica

2 cups fresh mangos
1 cup sugar
1 cup water
1 tablespoon lime juice
¼ teaspoon dried chili flakes

Peel and chop the mango – discard the pit.
Boil the mango in the water until tender. Add the sugar, lime juice, and chili flakes. Simmer until the mixture thickens. Cover and refrigerate.

Serves 2
Prep Time: approx. 5 Minutes
Cook Time: approx. 10 Minutes
Source: Ras Rody Organics

Pepper Wine - Jamaica

6 whole fresh hot red peppers
1 pint light rum, or dry sherry

Put the whole peppers into a glass jar and pour in the rum or sherry. Cover tightly with the lid and allow to stand for 10 days before using. Use a few drops in soups or sauce. Pepper vinegar is made in the same way. Makes about 1 pint.

If fresh peppers are not available, whole, hot dried peppers may be used.

Pickled Scotch Bonnet Peppers/Homemade Pickapep - Jamaica

20 scotch bonnet peppers
½ cup natural cane sugar
1 cup apple cider vinegar
½ cup water
¼ cup pimento berries
2 teaspoons fresh ginger, sliced
2 sprigs thyme
1 sterilized canning jar

Boil the scotch bonnet peppers in water for 10 minutes to temper its heat; strain.

Warm all the pickling ingredients together in separate pot until it reaches a boil.

Pour the warmed mixture over the peppers and place into a sterilized jar.

Seal and allow to pickle in a cool place for at least one week.

Serves 20
Prep Time: approx. 15 Minutes
Cook Time: approx. 10 Minutes
Source: Ras Rody Organics

Pineapple Jam - Jamaica

2 cups fresh pineapple
1 cup sugar
1 cup water
1 tablespoon lime juice
½ teaspoon grated ginger

Clean and finely chop the pineapple.
Cook the pineapple in the water until tender. Add the sugar, lime juice, and grated ginger.

Simmer until the mixture thickens.

Cover and refrigerate.

Serves 2
Prep Time: approx. 5 Minutes
Cook Time: approx. 10 Minutes
Source: Ras Rody Organics

Pineapple Sauce - Jamaica

1-cup fresh pineapple juice
5 leaves fresh basil
2 teaspoons lemon juice

In a saucepan heat pineapple juice, on medium bring to a boil then simmer till it reduces into a syrup.

Bruise and tear the basil leaves and add to sauce just before serving.

Prep Time: approx. 10 Minutes
Cook Time: approx. 20 Minutes
Source: Ras Rody Organics

Salsa Rojo para Frijoles Negros, Sweet Pepper Sauce for Black Beans - Cuba

This is an exceptionally good sweet pepper and tomato sauce dating back to the beginning of the century. Traditionally is served with Cuban black beans, but may be used with other dishes.

1 cup olive oil
1 ½ cups tomatoes, peeled and chopped
2 cloves garlic, crushed
¼ teaspoon black pepper
½ teaspoon Spanish (hot) paprika, or cayenne
¼ teaspoon oregano
½ teaspoon sugar
Salt to taste
½ cup tomato puree
2 cups pimientos, chopped and the liquid from the can
¼ cup vinegar, preferably cane vinegar

Heat the oil in a saucepan and add the tomatoes. Cook, stirring with a wooden spoon until the tomatoes have disintegrated, about 5 minutes. Add the rest of the ingredients, except the vinegar, and cook, stirring from time to time over low heat until the sauce is thick. Remove from the heat and stir in the vinegar.

Makes about 4 cups
Prep Time: approx. 15 Minutes
Cook Time: approx. 5 Minutes
Adapted from Source: The Complete Book of Caribbean Cooking

Sauce Vinaigrette, French Dressing – French Islands

¼ cup cane or white wine vinegar, or lime, or lemon juice, or a mixture of both
Salt
Freshly ground pepper
Pinch sugar
½ teaspoon Dijon mustard (optional)
¾ cup olive, or salad oil

Combine all ingredients in a bowl and whisk with a fork until the salt has dissolved. Or, place in a salad dressing bottle, close lid and shake vigorously till bended.

Variation:
¼ cup olive, or vegetable oil
2 tablespoons white wine vinegar
2 teaspoons prepared mustard, preferably Dijon
1 clove garlic, crushed (optional)
Salt, freshly ground pepper

Beat all ingredients together with a fork.

Makes about 1 cup
Prep Time: approx. 5 Minutes
Adapted from Source: The Complete Book of Caribbean Cooking

Sofrito - Cuba

2 tablespoons vegetable oil
1 medium onion, chopped
1 green bell pepper, seeded and chopped
5 cloves garlic, chopped
1 teaspoon salt
1/4 teaspoon pepper
1/4 teaspoon ground cumin
1 teaspoon dried oregano, crushed
2 bay leaves
2 tomatoes, chopped (optional)
3/4 cup canned tomato sauce

Heat oil in a skillet over medium-high heat. Add onion and garlic, and cook until onion is translucent. Add the bell pepper, and sauté until tender. Season with salt, pepper, cumin, oregano and bay leaves. Continue cooking until the mixture looks like a yummy green paste with oil around it. Stir in the tomatoes, if using, and cook stirring until all of the liquid is released. Gradually stir in the tomato sauce simmer until the sauce looks really red. Taste, and adjust seasonings if desired. Remove bay leaves.

Now the sauce is done. You can add it to Beans, rice, beans veggie burger or potatoes. Thin the sauce down if necessary with water, wine, beer, or whatever is handy. Authentic Cuban sofrito (sauce) to be added to Cuban dishes, stews and other things. This is where the different flavor of Cuban food comes from.

Serves: 6
Prep Time: approx. 15 Minutes
Cook Time: approx. 30 Minutes
Source: Allrecipes

Chapter 5

Grain & Pasta Dishes

- Akee Patties – Jamaica
- Almond Milk Rice – Jamaica
- Arroz Blanco, *White Rice* – Dominican republic
- Arroz con Ajo, *Garlic Rice* – Cuba
- Arroz con frijoles, *Rice with Beans* – Dominican republic
- Baked Mac and Cheese - Bahamian
- Beans and Rice, Jamaican Style
- Congis, *Red Beans and Rice* - Cuba
- Dal, *Split Pea or Lentil Puree* – Trinidad
- Frijoles Negros Pascuales, *Holiday Black Beans* – Cuba
- Frijoles Negros, *Black Beans* – Cuba
- Kwaku's Fungi
- Peas and Rice, Bahamian Style
- Pois et Riz Colles, *Rice and Beans Together* – Haiti
- Pois et Riz, *Peas and Rice* – Guadeloupe
- Rice and Peas – Jamaica
- Rice and Pumpkin - Jamaica
- Riz a l'aubergine, *Rice with Eggplant* - Haiti
- Riz au Djon-Dijon, *Rice with Black Mushrooms* – Haiti
- Riz Creole, *Rice Creole Style* – Martinique-Guadeloupe

Akee Patties – Jamaica

FILLING
2 cups fresh Ackee or 2 cans precooked Ackee
4 cups water, only for fresh Ackee
1 onion
½ teaspoon allspice
1 scotch bonnet pepper
2 tablespoons coconut oil

ROASTED PEPPER
2 sweet peppers
3 stalks scallion
1 scotch bonnet pepper
2 tablespoons coconut oil
5 leaves fresh basil

PATTIE DOUGH
4 cups bread flour
2 teaspoons baking powder
½ cup vegetable oil
1 cup water
½ teaspoon sugar

If using fresh ackee, boil in water for 20 minutes and strain Dice the onions and sauté in coconut oil for 5 minutes. Add the ackee, halved scotch bonnet pepper, and allspice. Cook together for another 10 minutes on moderate heat. Remove from pan and let the filling cool while preparing dough.

Rub peppers and scallion with oil and roast over open flame or on grill until charred.

Allow to cool in covered container, allowing peppers to steam to help with peeling.

Peel and de-seed the pepper, slice the peppers and scallions. Toss together with torn fresh basil leaves and let it cool while making the dough.

Mix flour and baking powder in a large mixing bowl. Add water slowly and combine with fingers to right consistency. Cut dough into 8 equal portions.

Roll into 1/8 inch thick flat rounds on floured surface. Add filling into the center of the rolled dough and fold end to end to form half circles.

Be careful to enclose all the filling and remove all air from within the cavity. Crimp the edges with a fork and cut for clean edge.

COOKING
1 cup coconut oil

Heat pan with coconut oil. Fry patties on both sides until dough is cooked and rich golden brown color. Serve with pickled scotch bonnet peppers.

Serves: 4
Prep Time: approx. 25 Minutes
Cook Time: approx. 10 Minutes
Adapted from Source: Ras Rody Organics

Almond Milk Rice – Jamaica

1 cup brown rice
6 cups almond milk
½ teaspoon all spice
½ cup shredded coconut
½ teaspoon orange zest
½ teaspoon vanilla
½ cup slivered toasted almonds

Rinse the rice in water until the water runs clear. Combine rice and milk in a saucepan and bring to a boil stirring often. Reduce heat and add the spices and salt.

Simmer until the rice is tender and creamy stirring often – this will take about 35 minutes.

Remove from the heat – stir in the sugar, coconut, orange zest, and vanilla.

Refrigerate until cool. Serve with slivered toasted almonds on top.

Serves: 4
Prep Time: approx. 15 Minutes
Cook Time: approx. 35 Minutes
Adapted from Source: Ras Rody Organics

Arroz Blanco, White Rice – Dominican Republic

2 cups long grain rice
1 large lime juiced
3 cups water
1 teaspoon salt
¼ cup peanut oil

Wash the rice thoroughly. Drain, cover with cold water, add the lime juice and allow to stand for 2 or 3 minutes. Drain. Pour the water into a heavy saucepan with tight fitting lid, add the salt, bring to a boil and pour in the rice. Stir, bring back to a boil, cover, lower the heat and cook for 10 minutes. Stir the oil into the rice, cover and cook on the lowest possible heat until the rice is tender.

Serves: 6
Prep Time: approx. 5 Minutes
Cook Time: approx. 35 Minutes
Adapted from Source: The Complete Book of Caribbean Cooking

Arroz con Ajo, Garlic Rice – Cuba

4 tablespoons unsalted butter
2 cloves garlic, crushed
2 cups long-grain rice
4 cups vegetable stock
Salt and Pepper to taste

Heat the butter in a heavy saucepan, add the garlic, stir, and add the rice and cook, stirring constantly, until the butter has been absorbed. Take care not to let the rice brown. Add the stock, season to taste, cover, bring to a boil then reduce the heat as low as possible and cook until the rice is tender and all the liquid is absorbed, 20 to 30 minutes.

Serves: 6
Prep Time: approx. 15 Minutes
Cook Time: approx. 35 Minutes
Adapted from Source: The Complete Book of Caribbean Cooking

Arroz con frijoles, Rice with Beans – Dominican Republic

3 ½ cups coconut milk
1 fresh hot pepper seeded and chopped
3 cloves garlic, minced
2 medium tomatoes, peeled, seeded and chopped
Salt to taste
1 tablespoon fresh coriander, chopped
2 cups long-grain rice
1 cup cooked red kidney beans

Pour ½ cup of coconut milk into a heavy saucepan with a tight fitting lid. Add the hot pepper, garlic, tomatoes, coriander and salt to taste. Cook, stirring, over low heat for 3 to 4 minutes or until the mixture is well blended. Stir in the rice, the beans and the 3 cups coconut milk. Stir gently, then cover and cook over low heat until the rice is tender and the liquid absorbed.

Serves: 6
Prep Time: approx. 15 Minutes
Cook Time: approx. 35 Minutes
Adapted from Source: The Complete Book of Caribbean Cooking

Baked Mac and Cheese - Bahamian

1 lb. uncooked elbow macaroni
1/2-cup butter
2 (16 ounce) bags cheddar cheese
1/2 large green bell pepper, diced
1/2 large white onion, diced
4 eggs
Black pepper
2 pinches salt
2 teaspoons paprika
1 habanero pepper, diced
12 ounces evaporated milk

Preheat oven to 375°F.
Add 2 pinches of salt to large pot of water. Bring water to a boil and add uncooked macaroni pasta. Boil until tender. Strain macaroni and place back in pot. Add butter and stir in macaroni until butter melts. Slowly stir in most of cheese evenly. Reserve 8 ounces (or half of a 16 ounce bag) for later topping. Add paprika, black pepper, onion, bell pepper, and 1/2 of a finely diced habanero or goat pepper. Stir well until cheese is melted and blended.

Beat eggs lightly and stir into mixture. Slowly add evaporated milk, pouring about half a cup at a time. Stir well, and spread the mixture evenly into a large prepared baking pan about 13 x 9. Top with remainder of cheese and loosely cover with foil.
Bake at 375°F for 1 hour to 1 hour 10 minutes or until top is a golden color. Allow macaroni to cool for 45-50 minutes until room temperature before serving.

Serves: 6
Prep Time: approx. 25 Minutes
Cook Time: approx. 70 Minutes
Adapted from Source: Kev's Bahamian

Beans and Rice, Jamaican Style

1 1/4 cups dry kidney beans
1-cup coconut milk
1 sprig fresh thyme
1 teaspoon minced garlic

1/8 cup chopped green onions
1 hot red chili pepper, sliced
2 1/4 cups uncooked brown rice

Combine beans and coconut milk in a large saucepan; cook for 2 hours on low heat. Stir in thyme, garlic, onions and 3 slices chili pepper; simmer for 7 minutes. Stir in rice and bring to a boil. Reduce heat, cover and simmer for 25 minutes, or until all liquid is absorbed and rice is tender.

Kidney beans are simmered in coconut milk and then cooked with rice, chili pepper and herbs.

Serves: 6
Prep Time: approx. 15 Minutes
Cook Time: approx. 50 Minutes
Source: Allrecipes

Congis, Red Beans and Rice - Cuba

2 tablespoons oil
1 medium onion, finely chopped
1 clove garlic, minced
1 green bell pepper, seeded and chopped
2 medium tomatoes, peeled, seeded and chopped
Salt, freshly ground pepper to taste
2 cups cooked California pink beans (frijoles colorados) or red kidney beans
1 cup raw rice
2 cups cold water

Heat the oil in a heavy, covered casserole or saucepan, add the onion and garlic, and sauté until the onion is tender but not browned. Add the pepper and tomatoes and cook, stirring, until the mixture is thick and well blended. Season to taste with salt and pepper.

Stir in the beans, mixing well. Add the rice and water mixing lightly. Cover and cook over very low heat until the rice is tender and all the water absorbed, about 20 minutes. The rice should be fluffy and dry.

Serves: 4-6
Prep Time: approx. 15 Minutes
Cook Time: approx. 35 Minutes
Adapted from Source: The Complete Book of Caribbean Cooking

Dal, Split Pea or Lentil Puree – Trinidad

2 cups split peas, or lentils
4 cups water
1 teaspoon ground turmeric
Salt
1 Medium onion, finely chopped
2 tablespoons coconut oil
2 cloves garlic, chopped
1 teaspoon cumin seeds

Soak the peas or lentils overnight, unless they are the quick cooking variety, in chick case omit this step. Add the turmeric to the peas and cook, covered, at a simmer until they are tender. Season to taste with salt and stir in the onion. Remove from the heat.

Heat the oil in a small pan and add the garlic and cumin. Sauté until the garlic is dark brown. Strain the oil into the peas. Stir, cover and let stand for a minute or two. Serve with boiled rice. The dal should have the consistency of mashed potatoes. If it seems to watery, simmer, uncovered for part of the cooking time.

Serves: 6-8
Prep Time: approx. 10 Minutes
Cook Time: approx. 35 Minutes
Adapted from Source: The Complete Book of Caribbean Cooking

Frijoles Negros Pascuales, Holiday Black Beans – Cuba

2 cups black beans
1 cup peanut oil
1 medium onion, finely chopped
4 cloves garlic, minced
1 fresh hot green pepper, seeded and chopped
½ teaspoon dried oregano, crumbled
½ teaspoon ground cumin
1 bay leaf
Salt to Taste
¼ cup cider or distilled white vinegar
4-ounce jar of pimientos and juice from jar
1 tablespoon sugar, or to taste
1 tablespoon cornstarch

Wash the beans thoroughly, drain, and place in a heavy, covered casserole or saucepan with 4 cups cold water. Cover and simmer gently until the beans are tender, 1 ½ to 2 hours, adding a little hot water from time to time as necessary. Heat the oil in a heavy frying pan and sauté the onion, garlic and pepper until the onion is tender, but not browned. Add the oregano, cumin and bay leaf, season to taste with salt and stir into the beans, which should have quite a lot of liquid. Cook, stirring from time to time, for half an hour longer then add the vinegar, the pimientos with their juice, and the sugar. Mix the cornstarch with a tablespoon of cold water and stir into the beans. Cook, stirring from time to time for 5 minutes longer. Serve with Salsa Roja para Frijoles Negros (Red Sauce for Black Beans).

Serves: 6-8
Prep Time: approx. 15 Minutes
Cook Time: approx. 35 Minutes
Adapted from Source: The Complete Book of Caribbean Cooking

Frijoles Negros, Black Beans – Cuba

Black beans with white rice are a great favorite in Havana, either served separately, or together as Moros y Cristianos (Moors and Christians).

2 cups black beans
4 cups cold water
¼ cup olive oil
1 medium opinion, finely chopped
1 clove garlic, minced
1 green bell pepper, seeded and chopped
1 bay leaf
Salt
Fresh ground pepper to taste

Wash the beans thoroughly, but do not soak them. Put them into a large saucepan with the cold water, cover and simmer gently until they are tender, about 1 ½ to 2 hours. Add a little hot water from time to time as necessary.

Heat the oil in a frying pan and add the onions, garlic, and pepper and sauté until the onion is tender but not browned. Add to the beans with the bay leaf and salt and pepper to taste. At this point the beans should still have quite a bit of liquid. Simmer, partially covered, for half an hour longer, stirring once or twice. Crush a spoonful or so of the beans to thicken the sauce, remove the bay leaf and serve. The beans should not be dry, but neither should the sauce be abundant.

Serves: 6 - 8
Prep Time: approx. 15 Minutes
Cook Time: approx. 90 Minutes
Adapted from Source: The Complete Book of Caribbean Cooking

Kwaku's Fungi

1/2 pot of water
8 okra
a pinch of salt
1 lb. of cornmeal

Slice up the okra, boil the water add okra with the salt. Add the cornmeal and turn for 2 hours with a turn stick. You can let it cook by itself at times; you can go to market and come back even. After 4 hours the fungi is ready. Eat with care, the fungi will be piping hot. If you na have okra, use cassie (cactus)

Serves: 2
Prep Time: approx. 15 Minutes
Cook Time: approx. 4 Hours
Source: Antiguan recipe

Peas and Rice, Bahamian Style

1/4 cup butter
2 ounces sliced tempeh, diced
1 large onion, diced
1 stalk celery, diced
1 large tomato, diced
1/2 (6 ounce) can tomato paste
1 tablespoon ketchup
Salt and pepper to taste
1 (15 ounce) can pigeon peas, with liquid
1 2/3 cups water
1 1/2 cups uncooked long-grain white rice
1 sprig fresh thyme, chopped

Melt butter in a large, heavy saucepan over medium high heat. Place tempeh in the saucepan, and cook until evenly brown. Stir in onion and celery, and cook until tender. Mix in tomato, tomato paste, and ketchup. Season with salt and pepper.

Reduce heat to low, and continue cooking about 15 minutes. Stir pigeon peas and their liquid, water, rice, and thyme into the saucepan. Bring to a boil, cover, and reduce heat. Cook 40 minutes on low, or until all liquid is absorbed. Fluff rice with a fork.

Peas and rice, often served under a tropical sun. You may have had it last while sitting on soft white sand, and looking at a clear blue sea. Goes excellently with other traditional Caribbean fare, such as Tofu curry or souse.

Serves: 4
Prep Time: approx. 15 Minutes
Cook Time: approx. 50 Minutes
Source: Allrecipes

Pois et Riz Colles, Rice and Beans Together – Haiti

1 cup California pink beans, or red kidney beans
2 tablespoons vegetable oil
1 medium onion, finely chopped
¼ cup chopped shallots
1 fresh hot green pepper, seeded and chopped
Salt to taste
2 cups long-grain rice
1 tablespoon unsalted butter

Put the beans into a large, heavy saucepan with water to cover by about 3 inches. Bring to a boil, cover and cook over low heat for until the beans are tender, 1 ½ to 2 hours. Drain, set the beans aside, and measure the liquid. There should be 4 cups. Add water to make up the quantity, if necessary, or if there is too much liquid, reduce it over brisk heat. Rinse out and dry the saucepan.

Heat the oil in the saucepan and sauté the onion, shallots and hot pepper and sauté until the onion is tender but not browned. Add the beans and season to taste with salt and cook, stirring, for a minute or two. Add the bean water, bring to a boil, pour in the rice, lower the heat, cover and cook until the water has evaporated and the rice is tender, about 20 minutes. Stir in the butter.

Serves: 6-8
Prep Time: approx. 15 Minutes
Cook Time: approx. 90 Minutes
Adapted from Source: The Complete Book of Caribbean Cooking

Pois et Riz, Peas and Rice – Guadeloupe

1 cup red beans or California pink beans
1 small onion
1 clove garlic, crushed
1 bay leaf
Sprig of Thyme
1 fresh, hot red or green pepper (optional)
1 ½ cups long-grain rice

Wash the beans thoroughly, drain and put into a heavy saucepan, large enough to hold both the beans and rice. Add the opinion, garlic, bay leaf, thyme and hot pepper, left whole. Add enough cold water to cover the beans by about 2-inches. Bring to a boil; lower the heat and cook, covered, at a gentle simmer until the beans are almost tender. If necessary add a little hot water from time to time.

Drain the beans. Reserve the liquid. Remove the bay leaf and pepper and discard. Measure the liquid and add enough water bring the quantity up to 3 cups. Return the beans and liquid to the saucepan. Wash to rice several times in cold water, drain, and then add to the beans. Stir once, then bring to a boil, lower the heat and cook, covered for 20 minutes, or until the rice is just tender and all the liquid absorbed.

Serves: 6-8
Prep Time: approx. 15 Minutes
Cook Time: approx. 90 Minutes
Adapted from Source: The Complete Book of Caribbean Cooking

Rice and Pees – Jamaica

1 cup brown rice
1 cup red peas
2 cups water
1 cup coconut milk
2 sprigs thyme
2 cloves

Soak the red peas overnight in water
Cook the peas in coconut milk, water, minced garlic, and thyme for 1 hour

Stir the rice into the peas and bring to a boil
Cover and let simmer on low heat for 30 minutes
Remove from heat once water is absorbed and rice is tender.

Serves: 4-6
Prep Time: approx. 15 Minutes
Cook Time: approx. 90 Minutes
Adapted from Source: Ras Rody Organics

Rice and Pumpkin - Jamaica

1 cup brown rice
1 cup pumpkin
2 cups water
½ cup coconut milk
1 teaspoon all spice
1 stick cinnamon bark

Cut the pumpkin into ¼ inch dice. Add all the ingredients into pot and mix together. Bring to boil over high heat.

Cover and let simmer for 30 minutes.

Remove from heat once water is absorbed and rice is tender.

Serves: 4-6
Prep Time: approx. 15 Minutes
Cook Time: approx. 90 Minutes
Adapted from Source: Ras Rody Organics

Riz a l'aubergine, Rice with Eggplant - Haiti

4 tablespoons sweet butter
¼ cup vegetable oil
2 pound eggplant, peeled and cut into ½ inch cubes
1 medium onion, finely chopped
2 cups long-grain rice
Salt to taste
1 ½ cups tomato puree
4 ounces grated Parmesan cheese

Heat the butter and oil in a large, heavy frying pan and sauté the eggplant cubes over high heat until they are golden brown, about 3 minutes. Set aside.

In a heavy, covered casserole sauté the onion until tender but not browned. Add 4 cups of water, bring to boil, pour in the rice, add salt to taste and stir. Cover and cook over very low heat until the rice is tender and all the liquid absorbed, 2- to 30 minutes.

Make a bed of the rice in an ovenproof platter, cover with the eggplant, pour the tomato puree over the eggplant, and then sprinkle with the cheese. Run under a broiler until the cheese melts and browns.

Serves: 6-8
Prep Time: approx. 15 Minutes
Cook Time: approx. 90 Minutes
Adapted from Source: The Complete Book of Caribbean Cooking

Riz au Djon-Dijon, Rice with Black Mushrooms – Haiti

The mushrooms used are Haitian black mushrooms, tiny, with inch-long inedible stalks. European dried mushrooms, such as German pfifferlinge, give almost the same taste to the dish, though it will lack the fine black color of the original.

1 cup dried mushrooms about 1 ounce
4 tablespoons unsalted butter
2 cups long-grain rice
2 cloves garlic, finely chopped
½ teaspoon thyme
Salt, freshly ground pepper

If using Haitian black mushrooms, remove the stems and soak them in 1 cup hot water. Soak the mushroom caps separately in another cup of hot water. If using European dried mushrooms, break them up coarsely and soak them in 2 cups hot water for half an hour. Discard the black mushroom stems, reserving the water, which will be richly colored as much of the color is in the stems. Drain the caps, reserving the water; drain the European mushrooms, reserving the water.
Heat the butter in a saucepan and sauté the rice with the garlic until the butter is absorbed. Add the reserved 2 cups of mushroom liquor plus 2 cups more water to the rice with the mushrooms, thyme, and salt and pepper to taste. Bring to a boil, cover, and turn the heat as low as possible. Cook for 20 to 30 minutes, or until all the liquid is absorbed and the rice is tender.

Serves: 4-6
Prep Time: approx. 15 Minutes
Cook Time: approx. 90 Minutes
Adapted from Source: The Complete Book of Caribbean Cooking

Riz Creole, Rice Creole Style – Martinique-Guadeloupe

2 cups long-grain rice
6 cups water
1 tablespoon salt

Wash the rice thoroughly in several waters. Drain. Put the 6 cups of water on to boil with the salt and when it comes to a rolling boil pour in the rice. Cook, uncovered, at a vigorous simmer for 15 minutes. Drain, rinse quickly under cold running water and return to the saucepan. Do not add any water. Cook, covered, over very low heat until the rice is tender and dry, about 20 minutes. Stir with two-pronged fork and serve. A matt is helpful in preventing the rice from catching.

Some cooks add 2 ½ times the volume of water to rice, (5 cups water to 2 cups rice), and cook the well-washed rice, covered, at a brisk simmer until the water has evaporated. The rice is then rinsed quickly in cold water, returned to the saucepan and put over very low heat, uncovered, to dry the grains.

Serves: 6-8
Prep Time: approx. 15 Minutes
Cook Time: approx. 60 Minutes
Adapted from Source: The Complete Book of Caribbean Cooking

Chapter 6

Vegetable & Salad Dishes

- Ackee Souffle – Jamaica
- Acrates d'aubergine, *Eggplant Fritters* – Martinique-Guadeloupe
- Acrates de chou palmist, *Palm Heart Fritters* – Martinique-Guadeloupe
- Alu Talkari, *Potato Curry* – Trinidad
- Asparagus Pudding – US Virgin Islands
- Aubergine a la Tomate, *Eggplant with Tomatoes* – Martinique
- Baked Pawpaw, *Papaya* – Jamaica
- Banane jaune avec sauce blanche, *Green Bananas with white sauce* – Martinique
- Berehein na forno, *Eggplant in Coconut Cream* – St. Maarten
- Breadfruit COO-COO – Barbados
- Breadfruit stuffed with Ackee – Jamaica
- Cassava Coo-Coo – Windward Islands
- Chou Palmiste en Sauce Blanche, *Palm Hearts in White Sauce* - – Martinique-Guadeloupe
- Christohene au Gratin, *Chayote with Cheese and Onion Stuffing* – Martinique
- Colombo de Giraumon, *Pumpkin Curry* – Martinique-Guadeloupe
- Concombre en Daube, *Stewed Cucumbers* – Martinique
- Concombres en Salade, *Cucumber Salad* – Martinique
- Conquintay coo-coo – Trinidad

- COO-COO
- Coo-Coo – Barbados
- Coo-Coo – Tobago
- Corn and Coconut Coo-Coo - Grenada
- Curried Vege Chunks
- Daube de Giraumon, *Seasoned West Indian Pumpkin* – Martinique-Guadeloupe
- Foo-Foo, *Pounded Green Plantain Balls* – Trinidad-Barbados
- Fried Okras – Jamaica
- Fried Ripe Plantains – All Islands
- Fruit Salad cups with lemon, mango and mint - Bahamas
- Funchi – *Corn Meal Pudding* – Netherlands Antilles
- Giraumon Boulli, *Boiled West Indian Pumpkin* – Martinique-Guadeloupe
- Key lime Honey Salad Dressing
- Key West Spinach & Jackfruit Salad
- La Salade de Leyritz, *Salad Leyritz* – Northern Martinique
- Matete de Fruit a Pain, *Sauted Breadfruit* – Guadeloupe
- Moros y Cristianos, *Moors and Christians* - Cuba
- Okra in Tomato Sauce – St. Croix
- Palm Heart & Papaya Salad - Caribbean
- Pepino en Salsa de Naranja, *Stewed Cucumbers in Orange Sauce* – Puerto Rico
- Quingombos Guisados, Stewed Okra – Puerto Rico
- Ratatouille Creole – Guadeloupe
- Roasted Breadfruit – Jamaica
- Sautéed Cabbage – Jamaica
- Steamed Callaloo – Jamaica
- Stuffed Cho-Cho, Chayote - Jamaica
- Stuffed Pawpaw, Papaya – Jamaica
- Sweet Corn Coo-Coo – Trinidad
- Sweet Potato Salad - Caribbean
- Temphe Pasta Salad - Caribbean
- Watercress Salad – Jamaica

Ackee Soufflé – Jamaica

3 tablespoons unsalted butter
3 tablespoons all-purpose flour
1 cup milk
½ teaspoon salt
½ teaspoon white pepper
1 teaspoon Worcestershire sauce
4 egg yolks
1 cup canned ackees, mashed to a puree
5 egg whites, stiffly beaten

Melt the butter in a heavy saucepan and stir in the flour. Cook stirring constantly with a wooden spoon for a minute or two, without letting the flour brown. Heat the milk and add all at once to the flour mixture. Cook, stirring until thick and smooth. Add the salt, pepper, and Worcestershire sauce. Remove from the heat and allow to cool a little.

Stir in the egg yolks one by one. Stir in the ackee puree. Stir in about a quarter of the egg whites, and then fold in the rest, gently but thoroughly. Pour into a buttered 6-cup soufflé dish mold. Bake in a 375° oven for about 30 minutes or until the soufflé is firm.

Serves: 4-6
Prep Time: approx. 15 Minutes
Cook Time: approx. 30 Minutes
Adapted from Source: The Complete Book of Caribbean Cooking

Acrates d'aubergine, Eggplant Fritters – Martinique-Guadeloupe

1 ½ pounds eggplant
1 egg, well-beaten
2 tablespoons milk
Salt, freshly ground pepper
1/8 teaspoon cayenne
1 cup all-purpose flour
1 teaspoon double-acting baking powder
Oil for deep frying

Peel the eggplant and cut into 1-inch cubes. Cook in boiling salted water until tender, about 15 minutes. Drain thoroughly and mash into a smooth puree. Add the egg, milk, salt, pepper and cayenne, mixing well. Sift baking powder with the flour and beat in the flour tablespoon by tablespoon into the eggplant mixture until smooth and light.

Deep fry by tablespoons in oil heated to 375 until golden brown. Serve hot.

Yields: about 18 fritters
Prep Time: approx. 15 Minutes
Cook Time: approx. 30 Minutes
Adapted from Source: The Complete Book of Caribbean Cooking

Acrates de chou palmist, Palm Heart Fritters – Martinique-Guadeloupe

14-ounce can palm hearts, drained and coarsely chopped
1 cup all-purpose flour
1 teaspoon double-acting baking powder
1 teaspoon salt
2 eggs, lightly beaten
1 medium onion, finely chopped
1 clove garlic, minced
2 fresh hot red or green peppers, seeded and chopped
1 tablespoon parsley, chopped
½ teaspoon thyme, crumbled
Salt, freshly ground pepper to taste
¼ cup milk, if necessary
Oil for deep frying

Sift together, into a large bowl, the flour, baking powder and salt. Stir in the eggs, onion, garlic, peppers, parsley, thyme, salt, pepper and the palm hearts, folding the ingredients lightly together to form a stiffish dough. Add the milk, if necessary. Allow the batter to stand for about one hour, the deep-fry by tablespoons in oil heated to 350°F to 375°F until golden brown. Drain on paper towels, keep warm and serve.

Yields: about 24 fritters
Prep Time: approx. 15 Minutes
Cook Time: approx. 30 Minutes
Adapted from Source: The Complete Book of Caribbean Cooking

Alu Talkari, Potato Curry – Trinidad

4 tablespoons coconut, or vegetable, oil
1 tablespoon fenugreek (optional)
2 cloves garlic, finely chopped
2 tablespoons masala (curry powder or paste)
2 pounds potatoes, peeled and sliced
1 small green mango, peeled and sliced (optional)
Salt
1 cup water

Heat the oil in a heavy frying pan or sauce pan and add the fenugreek, and the garlic cloves. Cook over medium heat, stirring with a wooden spoon, until the garlic is dark brown. Lift out, and discard the fenugreek garlic. Add the masala to the pan and cook, stirring, for 3 or 4 minutes. Add the potatoes, the green mango slices, salt to taste and the water. Cover and cook at a simmer until the potatoes are tender. If necessary, add a little water during the cooking, but the finished dish should be quite dry. This is very good as a stuffing for Roti, one of which makes a light lunch, supper or snack.

Serves: 4-6
Prep Time: approx. 15 Minutes
Cook Time: approx. 30 Minutes
Adapted from Source: The Complete Book of Caribbean Cooking

Asparagus Pudding – US Virgin Islands

This recipe is of Danish origin and is a good example of the pluralist nature of Caribbean cooking. Both foods and cooking methods illustrate the history of the islands.

8 tablespoons unsalted butter, plus butter for mold
½ cup all-purpose flour
Salt, white pepper
½ cup liquid from canned asparagus
½ cup milk
1 teaspoon onion juice
8 eggs
1 pound 3-ounce can asparagus, cut into ½- inch pieces

Thickly butter a covered quart mold. In a heavy saucepan melt the butter over low heat, stir in the flour and cook, stirring for 2 minutes without letting the flour color. Add salt, pepper, asparagus liquid, milk, and onion juice. Stir over low heat to make a smooth, thick sauce.

Off the heat beat in the eggs, one by one. Carefully fold in the asparagus. Pour into the mold. Cover the mold and set it in a large pan with hot water coming about halfway up the mold. Cover the pan and steam on top of the stove for 30 minutes, or until firm. Add a little boiling water to the pan during cooking, if necessary. Serve with Lemon Butter Sauce or Curry Sauce.

Serves: 6
Prep Time: approx. 15 Minutes
Cook Time: approx. 30 Minutes
Adapted from Source: The Complete Book of Caribbean Cooking

Aubergine a la Tomate, Eggplant with Tomatoes – Martinique

1 tablespoon vegetable oil or butter
1 onion, finely chopped
2 cloves garlic, chopped
1 eggplant, weighing about 1 pound, peeled and cut into 1-inch cubes
1 pound tomatoes, peeled and chopped
1 teaspoon chopped fresh hot red or green pepper
Salt

Sauté the onion in the oil or butter in a heavy casserole. Add the garlic and cook until the onion is tender but not browned. Add the eggplant and the tomatoes and cook; cover for 15 minutes longer, or until most the liquid has evaporated. Season with the hot pepper and salt to taste.

Serves: 4-6
Prep Time: approx. 15 Minutes
Cook Time: approx. 30 Minutes
Adapted from Source: The Complete Book of Caribbean Cooking

Baked Pawpaw, Papaya – Jamaica

Papaya is known as pawpaw in Jamaica. When ripe it is eaten as a fruit, when unripe as a vegetable.

1 green (unripe) papaya, weighing about 5 pounds
4 tablespoons unsalted butter
1 large onion, finely chopped
2 medium tomatoes, peeled and chopped
Salt, freshly ground pepper
1 cup bread crumbs
½ cup grated Parmesan cheese

Preheat oven to 400°F.

Cut the unpeeled papaya in half, lengthwise. Scoop out and discard the seeds. Drop the fruit into boiling water and cook until tender, 15 to 20 minutes. Lift out and drain. Carefully scoop out the flesh, reserving the shells. Heat 2 tablespoons of butter in a frying pan and sauté the onion until tender but not browned. Add the tomatoes, salt and pepper to taste and the mashed papaya. Mix thoroughly.

Stuff the shells with the mixture, sprinkle with the breadcrumbs and cheese, and dot with the remaining 2 tablespoons of butter.

Bake in a 400°F oven on a cookie sheet until the tops are browned.

Serves: 4-6
Prep Time: approx. 15 Minutes
Cook Time: approx. 30 Minutes
Adapted from Source: The Complete Book of Caribbean Cooking

Banane jaune avec sauce blanche, Green
Bananas with white sauce – Martinique

3 large green plantains, or 6 fairly small green bananas
3 tablespoons unsalted butter
3 tablespoons all-purpose flour
1 ½ cups milk
Salt, white pepper to taste
1/8 teaspoon grated nutmeg
½ cup grated Gruyere cheese (optional)

Peel the plantains or bananas by cutting through the skin lengthwise with a sharp knife in 3 places, then peeling off the skin. Cut the plantains in half cross-wise. The bananas should be left whole. Put into a saucepan with salted water to cover and cook until tender, about 30 minutes for the plantains, 15 minutes for bananas.

Heat the butter in a small saucepan and stir in the flour. Cook stirring constantly with a wooden spoon for a minute or two. Heat the milk and pour all at once into the butter flour mixture. Cook, stirring until the sauce is smooth and thick. Season to taste with salt and pepper; add the nutmeg. Arrange the bananas or plantains in a serving dish and pour the sauce over them.

Optional; ½ cup grated Gruyere cheese may be added to the white sauce, stirred in with the seasonings.

Serves: 4-6
Prep Time: approx. 15 Minutes
Cook Time: approx. 30 Minutes
Adapted from Source: The Complete Book of Caribbean Cooking

Berehein na forno, Eggplant in Coconut Cream – St. Maarten

1 large eggplant, weighing about 1-pound
1 tablespoon butter, softened
3 large onions, finely chopped
1 teaspoon dried hot red peppers, crumbled, or
1 fresh hot red pepper, seeded and chopped
Salt, freshly ground pepper
2 cups coconut cream

Peel the eggplant and slice thinly. Butter an ovenproof dish and arrange the eggplant slices in it. Cover with onions, sprinkle with peppers, season to taste with salt and pepper and pour the coconut cream over it. Cover the dish with a lid, or with foil, and bake in a 350°F oven for 45 minutes. Uncover and bake for 10 minutes longer.

Serves: 4-6
Prep Time: approx. 15 Minutes
Cook Time: approx. 60 Minutes
Adapted from Source: The Complete Book of Caribbean Cooking

Breadfruit COO-COO – Barbados

1 breadfruit, about 2-pounds, or a 1-pound 10-ounce can
½ pound tempeh coarsely chopped
1 onion, finely chopped
½ teaspoon thyme
1 bay leaf
1 sprig parsley
2 or 3 stalks of chives
6 tablespoons unsalted butter
Salt, freshly ground pepper to taste
A little vegetable stock

Peel the breadfruit, cut out the core, and cut up roughly. If using canned breadfruit, drain and chop coarsely. Put on to cook with the tempeh and onion, with the thyme, bay leaf, parsley, and chive tied up in piece of cheesecloth, in enough water to cover. Cook until the breadfruit is tender.

Drain, remove and card bouquet garni and mash in 4 tablespoons of the butter, over very low heat, adding a little vegetable stock to achieve a smooth texture with the consistency of rather stiff mashed potatoes. Season to taste with salt and pepper.

Turn into a buttered basin to mold, then turn out onto a warmed serving platter. Garnish with the remaining 2 tablespoons of butter.

Serves: 4-6
Prep Time: approx. 10 Minutes
Cook Time: approx. 30 Minutes
Adapted from Source: The Complete Book of Caribbean Cooking

Breadfruit stuffed with Ackee – Jamaica

2 cups quinoa
4 cups vegetable stock
2 dozen fresh ackees, or 1-pound 2-ounce can
1 large onion, finely chopped
1 breadfruit, peeled, or 1-pound 10-ounce can breadfruit, drained and mashed
Salt
Pepper
Butter

Preheat oven to 350°F.

Cook the quinoa with 4 cups vegetable stock. Add the fresh ackees and simmer until tender.

Bake the fresh breadfruit in a 350°F oven until tender, about 45 minutes. Allow to cool a little. Remove the core and, if necessary a little of the flesh from the stem end. Stuff with the quinoa mixture. Rub more butter on the outside and return to the oven for about 15 minutes, or until heated through.

If using canned breadfruit, line a buttered casserole with the mashed breadfruit, fill with the quinoa mixture, and top with more breadfruit. Dot with butter and bake in 350°F oven for 30 minutes, or until heated through.

Serves: 4-6
Prep Time: approx. 15 Minutes
Cook Time: approx. 45-60 Minutes
Adapted from Source: The Complete Book of Caribbean Cooking

Cassava Coo-Coo – Windward Islands

This dish occurs in Brazil as Angu de Farinha de Mandioca. Since cassava (manihot utilissima) is originally from Brazil and was taken to the Asiatic tropics by the Portuguese in the 17th Century, this is obviously a dish native to the Indians of Brazil, and it may well have spread to the Caribbean long before the West discovered the Americas.

6 cups water
2 cups cassava meal
Salt to taste

Bring the water to boil in a heavy saucepan, add salt and pour in the cassava meal in a slow, steady stream. Cook, stirring constantly with a wooden spoon, until the mixture is thick and smooth, about 10 minutes.

Serve as a starchy vegetable.

Serves: 4-6
Prep Time: approx. 5 Minutes
Cook Time: approx. 10 Minutes
Adapted from Source: The Complete Book of Caribbean Cooking

Chou Palmiste en Sauce Blanche, Palm Hearts in White Sauce – Martinique-Guadeloupe

2 14-ounce cans palm hearts
3 tablespoons sweet butter
3 tablespoons all-purpose flour
1 cup milk
½ cup heavy cream
Salt, white pepper to taste
½ cup freshly grated Parmesan or Gruyere cheese

Heat the palm hearts in their own liquid. Drain thoroughly and chop coarsely. Place in a buttered ovenproof dish.

Meanwhile melt the butter in a small saucepan, stir in the fould and cook over low heat, stirring constantly for about a minute. Heat the milk and cream together and pour on to the butter flour mixture, stirring constantly until smooth. Season to taste with salt and pepper and pour over the palm hearts. Top with the grated cheese and run under a broiler until the cheese is lightly browned.

Variation: Heat the palm hearts, cut into lengthwise pieces and serve with a freshly made tomato sauce and freshly grated Parmesan or Gruyere cheese.

Serves: 4-6
Prep Time: approx. 5 Minutes
Cook Time: approx. 30 Minutes
Adapted from Source: The Complete Book of Caribbean Cooking

Christohene au Gratin, Chayote with Cheese and Onion Stuffing – Martinique

3 large chayotes, each weighing about ¾ pound
5 tablespoons unsalted butter
1 large onion, finely chopped
Salt, freshly ground pepper
1 cup plus 3 tablespoons grated Parmesan cheese

Preheat oven to 350°F.
Boil the whole chayotes in salted water until tender, about 30 minutes. Remove from the saucepan, and when cool enough to handle, cut into halves lengthwise. Scoop out the pulp, including the edible seed, mash and set aside. Reserve the shells.

    Heat 3 tablespoons of the butter in a frying pan and sauté the onion until tender but not browned. Add the mashed chayote pulp, salt and pepper to taste and cook, stirring, for a few minutes to dry the mixture out a little. Off the heat, add the cup of cheese, stirring to mix well. Stuff the shells with the mixture, dot with the remaining 2 tablespoons butter and sprinkle with the extra cheese. Place on a baking sheet and bake in a 350°F oven for 15 minutes, or until the tops are lightly browned.

    Variation: This vegetable is also popular as a salad in Martinique. For Christophone en Salade (Chayote Salad), peel 2 large chayotes and cut lengthwise into 4 pieces. Do not remove edible seed. Boil in salted water for 20 minutes, or until tender. Drain thoroughly and when cool cut into ½-inch crosswise slices and toss gently with Sauce Vinaigrette, and ½ cup chopped shallots. Serve on lettuce leaves.

Serves: 4-6
Prep Time: approx. 15 Minutes
Cook Time: approx. 60 Minutes
Adapted from Source: The Complete Book of Caribbean Cooking

Colombo de Giraumon, Pumpkin Curry – Martinique-Guadeloupe

2 tablespoons vegetable oil
2 tablespoons unsalted butter
¼ pound tempeh, chopped
1 medium onion, chopped
1 bell pepper, seeded and chopped
1 teaspoon curry powder
¼ teaspoon curry powder
2 medium tomatoes, peeled and chopped
1 pound West Indian pumpkin (calabaza), or use Hubbard squash, peeled and cut into 1-inch cubes
Salt, freshly ground pepper to taste
1 large clove garlic, crushed

Heat oil and butter in a heavy saucepan; add the tempeh, onion and pepper and cook, stirring from time to time, until the onion is tender but not browned. Add the curry powder and cook, stirring for a minute or two. Add the cloves, tomatoes, pumpkin, salt and pepper, stir to mix, cover and cook on the lowest possible heat, stirring occasionally to prevent the mixture from burning.

When the pumpkin is very tender and almost reduced to a puree, stir in the garlic and cook, uncovered for a minute or so longer.

Serves: 4-6
Prep Time: approx. 5 Minutes
Cook Time: approx. 30 Minutes
Adapted from Source: The Complete Book of Caribbean Cooking

Concombre en Daube, Stewed Cucumbers – Martinique

3 medium sized cucumbers
3 tablespoons olive, or vegetable, oil
1 medium onion, finely chopped
1 pound tomatoes, about 3 medium, peeled and chopped
Salt, freshly ground pepper
Pinch sugar

Peel the cucumbers and cut in to halves, lengthwise. Scrape out the seeds and cut the cucumbers into 1-inch crosswise slices. Set aside.

Heat the oil in a saucepan and sauté the onion until tender but not browned. Add the tomatoes, salt and pepper to taste, and sugar. Add the cucumbers, stir to mix, cover and simmer very gently for 45 minutes.

Serves: 4-6
Prep Time: approx. 5 Minutes
Cook Time: approx. 55 Minutes
Adapted from Source: The Complete Book of Caribbean Cooking

Concombres en Salade, Cucumber Salad – Martinique

2 medium –sized cucumbers
1 teaspoon salt
1 large clove garlic, crushed
1 tablespoon lime, or lemon juice
1 or 2 teaspoons fresh hot pepper, seeded and finely chopped

Peel the cucumbers and cut into halves lengthwise. Scrape out the seeds. Chop the cucumbers coarsely and mix with the salt. Allow to stand for 10 minutes, and then drain thoroughly. Toss with the garlic, lime juice and hot peppers.

Serves: 4
Prep Time: approx. 15 Minutes
Adapted from Source: The Complete Book of Caribbean Cooking

Conquintay coo-coo – Trinidad

This is made with plantain flour, sometimes available in Health Food stores and specialty shops, often sold as banana flour. However, it is easy enough to make at home.

1 cup conquintay flour
1 cup water
Salt to taste
4 tablespoons butter

Bring the water to a boil, add salt, remove from heat and gradually pour in the conquintay flour, stirring all the time with a wooden spoon until thick and smooth. Return to heat and bring to a boil, stirring constantly. Cook for 2 to 3 minutes. Stir in the butter and serve.

To make the flour, peel and slice green plantains, place on a cookie sheet and dry in a very slow oven until they are quite crisp. Put through a food mill or grate in an electric blender as fine as possible. Sift through a hair sieve. Store in a covered glass jar.

Serves: 4-6
Prep Time: approx. 5 Minutes
Cook Time: approx. 10 Minutes
Adapted from Source: The Complete Book of Caribbean Cooking

COO-COO

Though Coo-Coo is traditionally credited to Barbados, it turns up in a great many islands including Jamaica, Trinidad, and Tobago. In the Netherlands Antilles and the Virgin Islands it is called Funchi or Fungi, and is cooked without the okras, sometimes even without butter, though this produces a rather dull dish. There is also a sweet fungi, popular in the Virgin Islands (see desserts).

Coo-Coo in Barbados is served as a starchy vegetable and sometimes with tomato sauce. The word coo-coo means a cooked side dish, and in addition to corn meal coo-coo there are Conquintay (plantain flour) Coo-Coo, Breadfruit Coo-Coo, Cassava Coo-Coo, and interesting cornmeal and coconut version from Grenada, and one from Trinidad made with fresh sweet corn.

Cold Coo-Coo can be cut into slices and fried in butter or vegetable oil.

Coo-Coo – Barbados

12 small, young okras
6 cups water
Salt to taste
2 cups yellow corn meal
3 tablespoons unsalted butter

Wash the okras, cut off stems and slice crosswise, about ¼ inch thick. Bring the water to a boil; add salt and okras and cook, covered, for 10 minutes. Pour the corn meal into the water and okras in a slow, steady stream, stirring with a wooden spoon.

Cook, stirring constantly, over medium heat until the mixture is thick and smooth, about five minutes. Turn into a greased basin to mold, then turn out onto a warmed serving platter and spread the butter on top, or turn out directly onto a warmed platter without molding. Serve hot.

Serves: 4-6
Prep Time: approx. 5 Minutes
Cook Time: approx. 15 Minutes
Adapted from Source: The Complete Book of Caribbean Cooking

Coo-Coo – Tobago

12 small, young okras
6 cups vegetable stock
Salt to taste
2 cups yellow corn meal
2 tablespoons unsalted butter
1 pound sweet potatoes, peeled, cooked and sliced
2 medium tomatoes, peeled and sliced
2 pimientos, sliced
Lettuce for garnish

Wash the okras, cut off stems and slice crosswise, about ¼-inch thick. Bring the stock to a boil, add salt to taste, and add okras, and cook, covered for 10 minutes. Pour the corn meal into the water and okras in a slow steady stream, stirring with a wooden spoon. Cook, stirring constantly, over medium heat until the mixture is thick and smooth, about five minutes.

Put the butter into a warmed basing, add the coo-coo and shake until it forms a ball and absorbs the butter. Turn onto a warmed serving platter and decorate with the sweet potatoes, tomatoes, pimientos and lettuce.

Serves: 4-6
Prep Time: approx. 5 Minutes
Cook Time: approx. 15 Minutes
Adapted from Source: The Complete Book of Caribbean Cooking

Corn and Coconut Coo-Coo - Grenada

4 cups freshly made coconut milk
Salt to taste
2 cups yellow corn meal

Put the coconut milk on to boil with salt to taste in a heavy saucepan. When boiling pour in the corn meal in a slow, steady stream, stirring constantly with a wooden spoon. Cook until the mixture is thick and smooth.

Serves: 4-6
Prep Time: approx. 5 Minutes
Cook Time: approx. 15 Minutes
Adapted from Source: The Complete Book of Caribbean Cooking

Curried Vege Chunks - Jamaica

1 pound vege chunks or seitan
1 small onion
2 tablespoons fresh ginger
1 small celery root
2 carrots
2 teaspoons fresh turmeric or 2 teaspoons curry powder
1 cup coconut milk
½ cup water

Cook vege chunks in coconut milk and water over moderate heat for 15 minutes.
Dice onion, carrots, and celery into ¼ inch cubes and grate the ginger into paste.

Cook grated turmeric into coconut oil for 2 minutes to extract color. If using dried curry powder, do not add until after the vegetables are sautéed.

Add diced vegetables and sauté over moderate heat for 10 minutes. Add cooked vege chunks with its liquid and simmer for 30 minutes to let the turmeric flavor the entire dish, careful not to over reduce the coconut milk. Serve with brown rice.

Serves: 4-6
Prep Time: approx. 5 Minutes
Cook Time: approx. 15 Minutes
Adapted from Source: Ras Rody Organics.

Daube de Giraumon, Seasoned West Indian Pumpkin – Martinique-Guadeloupe

1 ½ -pound West Indian pumpkin (calabaza), or use Hubbard squash
2 tablespoons all-purpose flour
¼ cup vegetable oil
4 ounces tempeh cut into cubes
2 cloves garlic, minced
1 tablespoon parsley, finely chopped
½ teaspoon marjoram
½ teaspoon thyme
1 bay leaf
Salt, freshly ground pepper
1 tablespoon white wine vinegar

Peel the pumpkin and cut into 1-inch cube. Toss the pumpkin pieces in the flour, using up all the flour. Heat the oil in a heavy saucepan and add the pumpkin pieces and the tempeh. Sauté for about 10 minutes stirring from time to time.

Add the garlic, parsley, marjoram, thyme, bay leaf, salt and pepper, and sauté for a minute or two longer. Add 1 ½ cups of hot water, half a cup at a time, stirring occasionally, and cook with the saucepan partially covered, until the pumpkin is tender and there is a fairly thick sauce. Just before serving stir in the vinegar. Serve as a starchy vegetable.

Serves: 4-6
Prep Time: approx. 5 Minutes
Cook Time: approx. 15 Minutes
Adapted from Source: The Complete Book of Caribbean Cooking

Foo-Foo, Pounded Green Plantain Balls – Trinidad-Barbados

3 green plantains, unpeeled
Salt

Cook the plantains in unsalted water until tender, about half an hour. When soft, peel, chop coarsely, and pound in a mortar until smooth, moistening the pestle with water from time to time as it gets sticky. Season with salt to taste, and form into small balls. Keep warm. Serve with Callaloo or any creole soup.

Serves: 4-6
Prep Time: approx. 5 Minutes
Cook Time: approx. 15 Minutes
Adapted from Source: The Complete Book of Caribbean Cooking

Fried Okras – Jamaica

20 large okras, quartered
1 cup flour, fine ground
2 tablespoons corn starch
2 teaspoons baking powder
1 ¼ cups sparkling water
5 basil leaves fresh

Mix flour, corn starch, and baking powder together. Whisk in water until a smooth and light batter is formed.

Drench okras and fresh basil in batter, careful to remove any excess.

Fry in two batches in 350°F oil until golden brown and crispy.

Squeeze fresh lime juice on fried okras just before serving.

Serves: 4-6
Prep Time: approx. 5 Minutes
Cook Time: approx. 15 Minutes
Adapted from Source: Ras Rody Organics

Fried Ripe Plantains – All Islands

When plantains are ripe their skins are quite black, but they must still be cooked before they can be eaten. They are served fried, though some dishes, such as Picadillo in Cuba, they are traditional. In Guadeloupe they are often served as a dessert, in which case they are sprinkled with sugar after they are fried, then flamed with *rhum vieux*. In French they are bananas frites, in the Spanish-speaking islands, platano frito.

3 large, ripe plantains
Butter, or vegetable oil

Cut off both ends of the plantains, peel and halve lengthwise. Ripe plantains can usually be peeled as easily as ripe bananas. If there is any difficulty, cut through the skins lengthwise on the ridges, with a small, sharp knife, and peel the segments. Slice the plantains in halves lengthwise, giving 12 slices in all. Heat the butter or oil in a large, heavy frying pan and sauté the pieces until browned on both sides. Drain on paper towels and serve immediately

If bananas are used as a substitute, use them when are ripe, but still firm and the skins are yellow, not black.

Serves: 4-6
Prep Time: approx. 5 Minutes
Cook Time: approx. 15 Minutes
Adapted from Source: The Complete Book of Caribbean Cooking

Fruit Salad cups with lemon, mango and mint - Bahamas

1 pineapple cut into bite size chunks
1 pint of blueberries
2 ripe mangos, cut into chunks
1 papaya, cut into chunks
3 sprigs fresh mint leaves
½ lemon juice
½ teaspoon lemon zest
2 oranges, cut into sections
2 cups mango juice

Cut pineapple, mango, papaya and orange into bite sized chunks. Place in a large bowl and mix in blueberries and mint. Add juice of half a lemon and ¼ teaspoon lemon zest, and mango juice. Toss and let stand in refrigerator for 30 minutes to mix flavors. Dish out fruit into 6 ounce cups and cover with liquid. Garnish with a mint leaf on top.

Serves: 4-6
Prep Time: approx. 10 Minutes
Chill Time: approx. 30 Minutes
Source: DL Phelps

Funchi – Corn Meal Pudding – Netherlands Antilles

4 cups water
1 tablespoon salt
2 cups yellow corn meal
4 tablespoons sweet butter

Bring the water and salt to a rolling boil, pour in the corn meal in a slow, steady stream and cook, stirring, over medium heat until the corn meal is thick and smooth, about 5 minutes. Beat in the butter, and turn out o to a warmed serving dish.

Serves: 4-6
Prep Time: approx. 5 Minutes
Cook Time: approx. 5 Minutes
Adapted from Source: The Complete Book of Caribbean Cooking

Giraumon Boulli, Boiled West Indian Pumpkin – Martinique-Guadeloupe

1 ½ pounds West Indian pumpkin (calabaza) or use Hubbard squash
Salt
2 tablespoons vegetable oil
2 cloves garlic, chopped
4 scallions chopped, using green and white parts
¼ teaspoon thyme
1 fresh hot red or green pepper, seeded and chopped
2 basil leaves, chopped
Freshly ground pepper
½ cup buttered bread crumbs (optional)
½ cup grated Parmesan cheese (optional)

Peel the pumpkin, remove any seeds and string, cut into 1-inch slices and cook in salted water to cover until tender, about 20 minutes. Drain thoroughly and mash. Set aside.

Heat the oil in a saucepan; add the garlic, scallions, thyme, hot pepper, and basil. Sauté until the scallions are tender but not browned. Season to taste with salt and pepper, add the pumpkin, mixing thoroughly and cook until heated through.

Optional: turn into a buttered baking dish, sprinkle with the buttered bread crumbs and cheese and place under broiler until the cheese melts and browns. Serve as a starchy vegetable.

Serves: 4-6
Prep Time: approx. 5 Minutes
Cook Time: approx. 25 Minutes
Adapted from Source: The Complete Book of Caribbean Cooking

Key Lime Honey Salad Dressing

1 clove garlic, minced
½ cup olive oil
¼ cup key lime juice
2 T honey
2 T chopped red onion
Salt and fresh ground pepper

Whisk or blend with food whip or food processor until well emulsified.

Serve with greens. Goes well with a salad of mixed greens, pistachios, orange slices and mint.

Serves: 5
Prep Time: approx. 15 Minutes
Cook Time: approx. 30 Minutes
Source: Joyce LAFray, Key Lime Cookin'

Key West Spinach & Jackfruit Salad

3 cups fresh spinach - rinsed, dried and torn into bite-size pieces
2 cups leaf lettuce - rinsed, dried and torn into bite-size pieces
1 cup finely shredded cabbage
2 large oranges, peeled and segmented
1 red onion, sliced in rings
2 (6 ounce) cans Jackfruit
1/2 teaspoon orange zest
3 tablespoons orange juice
2 tablespoons balsamic vinegar
2 teaspoons olive oil
1 teaspoon fresh chopped tarragon

In a large bowl, combine spinach, lettuce, cabbage, oranges, and onions. Add Jackfruit, and gently toss until combined. Set aside. In a small jar with a tight-fitting lid, combine orange zest, orange juice, vinegar, oil and tarragon. Cover, and shake until well mixed. Pour orange dressing over spinach salad, and gently toss until salad is well coated.

A yummy spinach salad with an orange dressing.

Serves: 4-6
Prep Time: approx. 15 Minutes
Cook Time: approx. 30 Minutes
Adapted from Source: Allrecipes

La Salade de Leyritz, Salad Leyritz – Northern Martinique

4 green (unripe) bananas
Salt
Vinaigrette dressing
1 large tomato, peeled, seeded and coarsely chopped
1 medium cucumber, peeled and coarsely chopped
1 cup celery, sliced
2 medium carrots, scraped and shredded
1 medium avocado, sliced

Peel the green bananas by cutting through the skin, lengthwise, in 2 or 3 places, then peeling the skin off in sections. Put the bananas into a saucepan with enough cold, salted water to cover, and cook, covered until they are tender, 10 to 15 minutes. Drain, cool and cut crosswise into ½ inch slices.

Mix all the ingredients, except the lettuce, lightly together, with the vinaigrette dressing. Line a salad bowl with the lettuce and fill with the banana mixture.

Serves: 4-6
Prep Time: approx. 5 Minutes
Cook Time: approx. 15 Minutes
Adapted from Source: The Complete Book of Caribbean Cooking

Matété de Fruit a Pain, Sautéed Breadfruit – Guadeloupe

1 breadfruit, weighing about 1 pound, peeled and cut into 1-inch cubes, or use canned breadfruit
2 ounces tempeh cut into cubes
1 tablespoon chives, finely chopped
2 cloves garlic, crushed
1 teaspoon parsley, chopped
¼ teaspoon thyme
1 fresh hot red or green pepper, seeded and chopped
Salt, freshly ground pepper
1 tablespoon vegetable oil
1 tablespoon lime juice

Put the breadfruit into a heavy saucepan with the tempeh, and enough water to cover. Cook, covered at the gentle simmer until the breadfruit is half done, about 15 minutes. Add the chives, garlic, parsley, thyme, and hot pepper, salt and freshly ground pepper and continue cooking, partially covered until the breadfruit is tender. Add the oil and lime juice, and continue cooking for 5 minutes or so longer, stirring constantly with a wooden spoon. The breadfruit will partly disintegrate forming a thick, creamy sauce for the pieces of it that remain whole. Serve as a starchy vegetable.

Serves: 4-6
Prep Time: approx. 10 Minutes
Cook Time: approx. 25 Minutes
Adapted from Source: The Complete Book of Caribbean Cooking

Moros y Cristianos, Moors and Christians - Cuba

Leftover Frijoles Negros (black beans) may be used for this recipe.

2 tablespoons olive oil
1 medium onion, finely chopped
1 clove garlic, minced
1 small green bell pepper, seeded and finely chopped
2 medium tomatoes, peeled, seeded and chopped
Salt, freshly ground pepper
2 cups cooked black beans
1 cup raw rice
2 cups cold water

Heat the oil in a heavy, covered casserole or saucepan; add the onion, garlic and pepper and sauté until the onion is tender. Add the tomatoes and cook, stirring, until the mixture is well blended and quite thick. Season to taste with salt and pepper. Stir in the beans, mixing well. Add the rice and water, mixing lightly. Cover and cook over very low heat until the rice is tender and all the water is absorbed. This is often served with fried egg and fried, ripe plantains.

Serves: 4-6
Prep Time: approx. 10 Minutes
Cook Time: approx. 15 Minutes
Adapted from Source: The Complete Book of Caribbean Cooking

Okra in Tomato Sauce – St. Croix

1 pound young okra pods, or 2 10 ounce packages frozen okra
¼ cup olive oil
1 medium onion, finely chopped
1 clove garlic, chopped
1 clove garlic, chopped
1 green bell pepper, seeded and chopped
1 fresh hot green pepper, seeded and chopped
3 medium tomatoes, peeled and chopped or, 1 cup canned Italian plum tomatoes, drained
Salt
Pinch of sugar

Wash the okras, pat dry with paper towels, and cut off the stem ends. If using frozen okra, thaw completely and pat dry. Heat the oil in a heavy frying pan, and sauté the okra until lightly browned all over. Lift out with a slotted spoon and transfer to a saucepan. In the oil remaining in the pan, sauté the onion, garlic and peppers until the onion is tender and very lightly browned. Add the tomatoes, salt, and sugar, and cook until the mixture is well blended, 2 or 3 minutes. Pour the tomato mixture over the okra, stir to mix, cover and cook until the okra is tender, about 5 mintues.

Serves: 6-8
Prep Time: approx. 5 Minutes
Cook Time: approx. 15 Minutes
Adapted from Source: The Complete Book of Caribbean Cooking

Palm Heart & Papaya Salad - Caribbean

2 ripe papayas, sliced into 8 lengthwise slices each
2 firm ripe avocados, peeled and sliced lengthwise into 8 slices each
1 4oz can palm hearts drained and sliced
Lime rind to garnish
Dressing:
Juice of 1 lime
1 tsp. Dijon mustard
1 tsp. hot pepper sauce
1 clove garlic, minced
Salt and fresh ground pepper
4 teaspoons olive oil

Whisk dressing ingredients together and set aside.

Prepare papayas, avocados and palm hearts and arrange on 6 plates. Drizzle with dressing. Garnish with lime rind and serve immediately.

Serves: 4-6
Prep Time: approx. 5 Minutes
Cook Time: approx. 15 Minutes
Adapted from Source: The Complete Book of Caribbean Cooking

Pepino en Salsa de Naranja, Stewed Cucumbers in Orange Sauce – Puerto Rico

3 cucumbers, about 8-inches long
3 tablespoon butter
1 tablespoons flour
1 cup fresh orange juice, strained
Salt, freshly ground white pepper
1 teaspoon grated orange rind

Peel the cucumbers, cut in half lengthwise, scrape out the seeds with a spoon and cut into 1/2-inch crosswise slices. Drop into boiling water and cook for 5 minutes. Drain. Place in a warmed vegetable dish. Melt the butter in a small saucepan. Stir in the flour and cook without letting the flour take on any color, for a minute or two. Add the orange juice, stir and cook until smooth and thickened. Season to taste with salt and pepper, add rind, mix thoroughly and pour over the cucumbers.

Serves: 4-6
Prep Time: approx. 5 Minutes
Cook Time: approx. 15 Minutes
Adapted from Source: The Complete Book of Caribbean Cooking

Quingombos Guisados, Stewed Okra – Puerto Rico

1 ½ pounds young okra pods
1 recipe Sofrito

Was the okras and cut off the stem ends. If they are young and small, leave them whole, older pods should be cut into ½-inch slices. Combine the okras and Sofrito in a saucepan, cover and simmer for 15 to 20 minutes, or until the okra is tender.

Variation: Green beans may be cooked in the same way.

Serves: 4-6
Prep Time: approx. 5 Minutes
Cook Time: approx. 15 Minutes
Adapted from Source: The Complete Book of Caribbean Cooking

Ratatouille Créole – Guadeloupe

The special feature of this dish is the *gros concombre*, the enormous, light green cucumber of Guadeloupe and Martinique and some other islands. The cucumbers weigh a pound or more each but, apart from size, differ very little from our cucumbers, which can be used instead. Simply choose the biggest ones available.

½ cup olive oil
1 eggplant, weighing about 1 pound
1 or 2 large cucumbers, weighing about 1 pound
1 pound zucchini
1 pound tomatoes, peeled and sliced
½ pound green bell peppers, seeded and sliced
½ pound ripe red bell peppers, seeded and sliced, or sliced canned pimientos
1 teaspoon sugar
Salt, freshly ground pepper

Heat the oil preferably in an earthenware casserole, or use any heavy saucepan or casserole large enough to hold all the ingredients comfortably. Peel the eggplant and cut into crosswise slices ½-inch thick. Cut the widest of these in half. Arrange the eggplant slices in the casserole. If the cucumbers are waxed, peel them and cut into ½-inch crosswise slices; otherwise leave unpeeled. Add to the casserole with the zucchini, washed, with eh ends cut off, and sliced into ½-inch pieces. Add the tomatoes and the peppers. Season with the sugar, salt and pepper, cover and cook for 15 minutes. Uncover and cook for 15 minutes longer, or until most of the liquid has evaporated.

Serves: 6-8
Prep Time: approx. 5 Minutes
Cook Time: approx. 25 Minutes
Adapted from Source: The Complete Book of Caribbean Cooking

Roasted Breadfruit – Jamaica

1 breadfruit

Build an open fire pit.

Roast the whole breadfruit over open fire on all sides, up to 1 hour.

Peel or scrape charred skin and serve with stews.

Serves: 4-6
Prep Time: approx. 5 Minutes
Cook Time: approx. 60 Minutes
Adapted from Source: Ras Rody Organics

Sautéed Cabbage – Jamaica

2 cups cabbage
1 small onion
2 cloves garlic
2 teaspoons coconut oil
2 sprigs thyme

Shred cabbage on fine grater and slice onion and garlic.

Place all three ingredients into hot pan with coconut oil.

Sauté for 5 minutes until the cabbage begins to break down.

Finish with fresh picked thyme.

Serves: 4-6
Prep Time: approx. 5 Minutes
Cook Time: approx. 15 Minutes
Adapted from Source: Ras Rody Organics

Steamed Callaloo – Jamaica

1 bundle callaloo
1 small onion
2 teaspoon coconut oil
½ teaspoon all spice
½ scotch bonnet pepper, deseeded

Roughloo and slice onion.

Place all three ingredients into hot pan with coconut oil. Sauté together with allspice and sliced scotch bonnet pepper. Reduce heat to low and steam covered for 10 minutes until the callaloo is tender.

Serves: 4-6
Prep Time: approx. 5 Minutes
Cook Time: approx. 15 Minutes
Adapted from Source: Ras Rody Organics

Stuffed Cho-Cho, Chayote - Jamaica

3 large chayotes, each weighing about 3/4 –pound
2 tablespoons vegetable oil
1 large onion, finely chopped
1 clove garlic, chopped
1 pound tofu crumbles
1 tablespoon curry powder, or 1 fresh hot red pepper, seeded and chopped
3 medium tomatoes, peeled and chopped
Salt, freshly ground pepper
6 tablespoons grated Parmesan cheese
6 tablespoons bread crumbs
3 tablespoons sweet butter

Preheat oven to 350°F.

Boil the whole chayotes in salted water until tender, about 30 minutes. Remove from the saucepan, and when cool enough to handle, cut into halves lengthwise. Scoop out the pulp, including the edible seed, mash and set aside. Reserve the shells.

Heat the oil in a frying pan and sauté the onion, garlic and tofu crumbles, stirring from time to time. Add the curry powder or hot pepper, and cook for a few minutes longer. Add the tomatoes and the chayote pulp. Cook, stirring, until the ingredients are well blended, and the mixture is fairly dry.

Season well with salt and pepper, pack into the chayote shells, sprinkle with cheese and bread crumbs, dot with butter and bake in a 350° oven for 15 minutes, or until lightly browned.

Serves: 4-6
Prep Time: approx. 10 Minutes
Cook Time: approx. 45 Minutes
Adapted from Source: The Complete Book of Caribbean Cooking

Stuffed Pawpaw, Papaya – Jamaica

1 green (unripe) papaya, weighing about 5 pounds
2 tablespoons vegetable oil
1 large onion, finely chopped
1 clove garlic, chopped
1 pound tofu crumbles
3 medium tomatoes, peeled and chopped
1 fresh hot red or green pepper, seeded and chopped
Salt, freshly ground pepper
1 tablespoon sweet butter
4 tablespoons grated Parmesan cheese
Tomato Sauce or Brown Sauce

Wash the papaya, peel, cut in half lengthwise, and remove and discard the seeds. Drop the papaya halves into boiling, salted water and parboil for 10 minutes. Drain thoroughly and pat dry with paper towels.

Heat the vegetable oil in a frying pan and add the onion, garlic, and sauté for 15 minutes, stirring from time to time. Add the tofu crumbles, tomatoes, hot pepper and salt and pepper to taste and cook, stirring until the mixture is well blended and thick.

Arrange the papaya halves in a greased baking pan and fill them with the mixture. Sprinkle with grated cheese and dot with butter. Bake in a 350 oven for 30-40 minutes. Serve with Tomato Sauce or Brown Sauce served separately.

Serves: 4-6
Prep Time: approx. 10 Minutes
Cook Time: approx. 55 Minutes
Adapted from Source: The Complete Book of Caribbean Cooking

Sweet Corn Coo-Coo – Trinidad

12 small young okras
2 cups water
Salt to taste
2 cups fresh sweet corn, grated
2 tablespoons butter

Wash the okras, cut off the stems and slice crosswise, about ¼-inch thick. Bring the water to a boil; add salt and okras and cook, covered, for 10 minutes. Add the corn and cook, stirring, until the mixture is thick and creamy. Stir in the butter and serve hot.

Serves: 4-6
Prep Time: approx. 5 Minutes
Cook Time: approx. 15 Minutes
Adapted from Source: The Complete Book of Caribbean Cooking

Sweet Potato Salad - Caribbean

1 large russet potato, peeled and quartered
1 large sweet potato, peeled and quartered
1 cup corn
1 teaspoon prepared Dijon-style mustard
2 tablespoons fresh lime juice
3 tablespoons chopped fresh cilantro
1 clove garlic, minced
3 tablespoons canola oil
1/2 teaspoon salt
1/4 teaspoon ground black pepper
1 cucumber, halved lengthwise and chopped
1/2 red onion, thinly sliced
1/4 cup finely chopped peanuts

Place the russet potato pieces into a large saucepan, and cover with salted water. Bring to a boil, turn the heat down, and simmer for 10 minutes. Add the sweet potato, and cook about 15 minutes more. Remove a piece of each potato, and cut it in half to see if it is cooked enough. Once the potatoes are tender, add corn kernels; cook another 30 seconds. Drain through a colander.

Fill the saucepan with cold water, and drop vegetables into water. Cool for 5 minutes, and drain.

In a large bowl, whisk together mustard, lime juice, cilantro, and garlic. Slowly whisk in oil. Mix in salt and black pepper. Cut cooled potatoes into 1-inch cubes, and add to dressing along with cucumber, and red onion. Toss well. Serve at room temperature or chilled. Toss the peanuts in just before serving.

Serves 4-6
Prep Time: approx. 15 Minutes.
Cook Time: approx. 30 Minutes.
Source: Allrecipes

Tempeh Pasta Salad - Caribbean

3 cups uncooked rotini pasta
8 ounce tempeh
1 red bell pepper, julienned
1 mango - peeled, seeded and cubed
2 tablespoons chopped fresh cilantro
1 jalapeno pepper, seeded and minced
1 teaspoon lime zest
3 tablespoons fresh lime juice
2 tablespoons olive oil
1 tablespoon honey
1/2 teaspoon ground cumin
1/2 teaspoon ground ginger
1/4 teaspoon salt

Bring a large pot of lightly salted water to a boil. Add pasta and cook for 8 to 10 minutes or until al dente; drain and rinse under cold water. Place pasta, tempeh, red pepper, mango, cilantro and jalapeno in a large bowl and set aside.

In a small bowl, whisk together the lime zest, lime juice, olive oil, honey, cumin, ginger and salt. Pour over salad, toss to coat and let sit in refrigerator for at least one hour before serving.

Serves: 4-6
Prep Time: approx. 15 Minutes.
Cook Time: approx. 30 Minutes.
Adapted from Source: Allrecipes

Watercress Salad – Jamaica

2 cups fresh watercress leaves, picked and cleaned
½ cup heart of palm
4 tablespoons coconut oil
2 tablespoons lime juice
½ teaspoon acacia honey
½ teaspoon coriander seed

Rough cut callaloo and slice onion.

Place all three ingredients into hot pan with coconut oil.

Sauté together with allspice and sliced scotch bonnet pepper. Reduce heat to low and steam covered for 10 minutes until the callaloo in tender.

Serve as side dish as a healthful addition to the meal.

Serves: 4-6
Prep Time: approx. 5 Minutes
Cook Time: approx. 15 Minutes
Adapted from Source: Ras Rody Organics

Chapter 7

Breakfast Dishes

- Corn and Potato Cakes - Mexico
- Curried Tofu Scramble - Florida
- Good Morning Sunshine Frittata - Florida
- Herbed Avocado Toast - Florida
- Oatmeal with Cinnamon Sugar and Pecans - Florida
- Oven Roasted Potato with Rosemary - Florida
- Pineapple Papaya Salad with Dried Apricots & Coconut - Cuba
- Rice Porridge with Gingered Blueberries and Toasted Nuts - Cayman
- Savory Porridge with Vegetable -Trinidad

Corn and Potato Cakes - Mexico

2 medium potatoes, peeled and sliced 1/2 to 3/4 inches thick (about 1 lb.)
1/2 cup 1% low-fat milk, separated
1 (11 ounce) can corn (Mexican mix with peppers, if desired)
1 (4 ounce) can green chilies, diced
3/4 cup low-fat cheddar cheese, shredded (or low-fat Mexican cheddar and Monterey jack blend)
2 tablespoons flour
2 tablespoons cornmeal
1 1/2 teaspoons seasoning salt
1 teaspoon dried oregano
1/2 teaspoon garlic powder
1/4 teaspoon pepper
1 egg
2 tablespoons butter, separated
2 teaspoons butter, separated

Boil 2 quarts water and add sliced potatoes. Boil 15 minutes. Remove with slotted spoon and put potatoes through ricer. Add 1/4 cup milk to potatoes and mix well. Should make about 2 cups mashed potatoes. In large bowl, combine mashed potatoes, corn, chilies, cheese, flour, corn meal, seasoned salt, oregano, garlic powder and pepper. Mix well. Beat egg with 1/4 cup milk, add and mix well.
Heat non-stick skillet over medium low heat. Drop in 2 teaspoons butter. In batches, drop potato mixture onto skillet, 1/4 cup at a time, four times per batch. Carefully form into 3-inch rounds. Cook about 7-8 minutes, until golden brown, turning once.
Repeat 3 times. Place finished cakes onto cookie sheet and keep warm in 225° oven. Serve with hot sauce on the side, if desired.
Serves: 6
Prep Time: approx. 15 Minutes
Cook Time: approx. 30 Minutes
Adapted from Source: Genius Kitchen

Curried Tofu Scramble - Florida

1 tablespoon olive oil
16 ounces tofu
1 roma tomato, seeded and diced
1/2 cup mushroom, diced
3 scallions, sliced
1 1/2 teaspoons curry powder
1 teaspoon salt
1 dash cayenne pepper

Heat olive oil in a frying pan.

Crumble tofu with your hands and add to the pan. Stir for a couple of minutes.

Add the remaining ingredients. Stir and adjust the seasoning. Turn off the heat.

Infuse love into the food and serve immediately!

Serves: 4
Prep Time: approx. 15 Minutes
Cook Time: approx. 30 Minutes
Adapted from Source: Genius Kitchen

Good Morning Sunshine Frittata - Florida

1 Medium white potato grated
2 Stalks green onion chopped
4 Shallots
2 cloves of garlic (smashed in a press)
1 Tablespoon of garlic salt seasoning
1 cup cooked oatmeal
1 Zucchini squash grated
13 Farm fresh eggs
1 cup shredded cheese (cheddar, asiago, Monterey jack)
Olive oil
Salt
Pepper

Preheat oven to 400°F.
Grate potatoes, Zucchini and Shallots. Then sauté with Shallots, Garlic in a large cast iron skillet on the stovetop on medium to high heat. Brown till crispy on bottom. Add cooked oatmeal and press into a base layer. (This forms the crust of the frittata.)

In a large mixing bowl, whisk with a hand blender, eggs, green onions, garlic salt, until foamy. Salt and Pepper to taste. When base layer is crispy, spread a handful of grated cheese. Then pour egg mixture over base cook on medium high heat, till egg mixture is half set. Then add second half of cheese to top and place in oven for 20 min. at 400°F. Till top is brown and bubbly.

Serve warm garnish with a side of cream cheese, feta, garlic, and cucumber spread.

Serves: 6-8
Prep Time: approx. 15 Minutes
Cook Time: approx. 30 Minutes
Source: DL Phelps

Herbed Avocado Toast - Florida

2 slices gluten free bread, sliced thick
1 perfectly ripe avocado
1 1/2 teaspoons vegan mayonnaise (optional)
1 pinch salt
1 pinch freshly grated black pepper
1 pinch lemon juice
1 fresh sprig of rosemary

Scoop the avocado out of the skin into a bowl.
Mash the avocado with a fork (mash well to create a smooth spread, or just a few times for a chunkier version).
Toast your bread to perfection, spreading the vegan mayonnaise first and then the mashed avocado on top of each slice.

Top with a small pinch of salt and freely ground black pepper. Pull the leaves off the sprig of rosemary crush in your hands by rubbing hands together over the toast.

Optional: (A small splash of lemon juice).

Serves: 1
Prep Time: approx. 5 Minutes
Cook Time: approx. 5 Minutes
Source: DL Phelps

Oatmeal with Cinnamon Sugar and Pecans - Florida

1/4 cup oil
1/2 cup brown sugar
1 egg
1/2 cup chopped pecans
1 1/2 cups oatmeal
1/2 tablespoon baking powder
1/2 cup skim milk
1/4 teaspoon nutmeg
1/2 teaspoon cinnamon

Preheat oven to 350 degrees.

Combine oil, sugar, egg, and pecans in a medium bowl. Add oatmeal, baking powder and milk and stir until blended. Pour into a lightly greased 8x8-baking dish. Sprinkle with nutmeg and cinnamon.

Bake at 350 degrees for 30 minutes. Cut into squares and serve hot or cold with milk and/or fruit.

Serves: 4
Prep Time: approx. 5 Minutes.
Cook Time: approx. 30 Minutes.
Adapted from Source: Genius Kitchen

Oven Roasted Potato with Rosemary - Florida

2 cloves garlic
½ cup extra-virgin olive oil
3 tablespoons finely chopped fresh flat-leaf parsley
2 teaspoons chopped fresh rosemary
2 pounds (7 or 8 small) unpeeled Yukon Gold, white, or red potatoes, scrubbed
1½ teaspoons kosher salt
Grated zest from 1 lemon (1 tablespoon lightly packed), plus the juice

Preheat the oven to 450°F.

Finely chop the garlic and put it in a large bowl. Add the oil, parsley, and rosemary.

Cut the potatoes into ¾- to 1-inch-wide wedges.

Add the potatoes to the bowl and sprinkle with the salt. Toss with your hands to evenly coat the potatoes with the oil mixture.

Spread the potatoes on a large rimmed baking sheet, scraping the bowl of any extra oil and herbs, and arrange the potatoes with a flat side down. Roast until the bottom is golden, about 25 minutes. Top with the lemon zest.

Serve hot in a serving bowl add the bits of herbs and lemon juice on top.

Serves: 4-6
Prep Time: approx. 15 Minutes
Cook Time: approx. 30 Minutes
Source: DL Phelps

Pineapple Papaya Salad with Dried Apricots & Coconut - Cuba

1 papaya, peeled and diced 3/4-inch cubes (5 cups)
2 mangoes, peeled and diced 3/4-inch cubes (2 1/2 cups)
1 fresh pineapple, peeled and diced reserving the juice 3/4-inch cubes (4 cups)
2 large bananas, peeled and diced 3/4-inch cubes (2 cups)
1 cup dried apricots
1/4 cup fresh grated coconut, for garnish

Combine the papaya, mangoes, and pineapple in a large bowl and add the juice from the pineapple.

Cover and refrigerate until chilled.

Just before serving, add the bananas, dried apricots and garnish with fresh coconut.

Serves: 4-6
Prep Time: approx. 15 Minutes
Cook Time: approx. 0 Minutes
Adapted from Source: A taste of Home

Rice Porridge with Gingered Blueberries and Toasted Nuts - Cayman

1 cup uncooked rice
4 cups water
½ teaspoon sea salt
2½ cups milk
2 tablespoons chia seeds
1 tablespoon coconut oil

Gingered Blueberry Topping:
1¼ cups frozen blueberries
2 tablespoons maple syrup
1 tablespoon water
½-inch piece fresh ginger, grated
½ teaspoon fresh lemon juice
⅛ teaspoon sea salt

1 cup mixed nuts, chopped (use what you have on hand)
Bring the rice, water, and salt to a boil in a medium saucepan; cover the pot, turn the heat down, and simmer for 30 minutes, stirring occasionally. Turn the heat off and let the porridge sit for an hour (or overnight). Stir in the milk, chia seeds, and coconut oil and bring to a simmer over medium heat; turn the heat off, cover the pot, and let it sit for 10 minutes before serving.

Meanwhile, combine all ingredients for the topping in a small saucepan over medium heat. Cover the saucepan, bring it up to a boil, and let it cook for 3 minutes. Heat a heavy frying pan then toss the sliced nuts, stirring constantly for 3-5 minutes, until toasted.

Serves: 4-6
Prep Time: approx. 5 Minutes
Cook Time: approx. 30 Minutes
Source: DL Phelps

Savory Porridge with Vegetable - Trinidad

1-teaspoon oil
½ teaspoon cumin seeds
1 cup assorted bite size cut vegetables
1-teaspoon salt
½ teaspoon cumin powder
¼ teaspoon turmeric powder
1-cup plain rolled oats
3 cups water
Optional ingredients:
Ghee
Half boiled or hard boiled eggs
Freshly cracked pepper
Finely chopped fresh cilantro leaves

Place a heavy bottom pan on medium heat and drizzle the oil. When the oil heats up, scatter the cumin seeds and let it sizzle for a few seconds.

Drop the vegetables followed by ½ teaspoon salt, turmeric and cumin powder. Mix it and sauté for 1 minute.
Scatter the rolled oats, mix it around and pour the water. Sprinkle rest of the salt and bring the water to a boil. Then, bring the heat down to medium and let it simmer for 3 to 4 minutes or until the oats are cooked through and turns creamy.

Check for salt and add any, if required.
Serve warm by topping it with boiled eggs, drizzle of ghee, fresh cilantro and some freshly cracked black pepper.

Serves: 4-6
Prep Time: approx. 5 Minutes
Cook Time: approx. 15 Minutes
Adapted from Source: Playfulcooking.com

Chapter 8

Main Dishes

- Easy Soy Milk – DIY
- Easy Tofu - DIY
- Bahamian Style Grilled LOST HER
- Bahamian MA UNHI
- Jerked LOST HER with Coconut
- Grilled SALM - UN with Habanero Lime Butter
- Grilled Spiny LOST HER with Basil Butter
- Margarita MA UNHI Acapulco
- CrockPot Jerk Tofu
- Grilled Tofu with Fresh Mango Salsa
- Jays Grilled Tofu
- Key West Grilled Tofu
- Lechon Asado: Cuban Shredded Jackfruit

EASY SOY MILK - DIY

1 cup dry soy beans (preferably organic)
5 cups water (plus more for soaking and rinsing)
Optional sweetener to taste (like sugar, agave, maple syrup or stevia)

Soak the beans in fresh water for one or two days in a large container. Make sure there is enough room for the beans to expand to triple their size. Add water if the water level drops below the top of the beans.

Drain the beans and transfer to a large bowl. Add enough water to completely submerge the beans.

Rub the beans between your fingers to remove the skins. Remove the skins from the bowl by mixing the beans around and letting the beans settle to the bottom. Then skim the top to get at the loose skins. Discard the skins. Try to get most of the skins but don't worry if there are a few left.

Drain the beans.

Blend the beans with 5 cups of water until the beans well pureed. This took about one minute with my regular 12 speed Oster Blender on the Liquefy setting. If you have a high speed blender, take care not to over blend. You may need to work in a couple batches depending on your blender's capacity.

Strain the liquid into a large pot using a nut milk bag, jelly bag or a few layers of cheesecloth over a colander or sieve. The liquid will be your soy milk. The pulp, known as okara, can be discarded or used in other recipes.

Heat the milk on high heat until boiling while stirring regularly. The milk tends to form a skin at the bottom of the pot so stirring is necessary to keep this from building up.

During this process, a skin may form at the top; this is normal and known as yuba. The yuba can be stirred back into the milk or skimmed off.

Let the milk boil for a couple minutes; stir and reduce the temperature as needed to prevent the milk from bubbling over.

Reduce the heat to medium or medium low. At this point, it's a good idea to taste the milk. It may be a bit beany tasting and bitter. As the milk is cooked, the beany and bitter taste will be reduced. Let the milk simmer for anywhere between 10 minutes to 2 hours. How long is up to you.

When ready, strain the milk into a container.

Serve the milk hot or cold. Add sweetener to taste. I use about 1 or 2 teaspoons of maple syrup per cup.

NOTES
Store your fresh soy milk in the fridge for up to 3 days. The leftover soymilk pulp (okara) will also stay fresh in the fridge for about 3 days.

Yield: 5 cups
Prep time: 10 minutes
Cook time: 2 hours
Source: Mary's Test Kitchen

EASY TOFU - DIY

About 5 cups plain soymilk
1/2 cup water
1 1/2 tablespoons fresh lemon juice

Combine the water and lemon juice.

Separately, heat the soy milk to 160F in a large pot. Be sure to stir constantly to keep the soy milk from burning on the bottom. If you don't have a thermometer, you can bring it just to a boil, then remove from heat and stir for 2-3 minutes to cool.

Remove the soy milk from heat and stir half of the lemon mixture into the soy milk for 1 or 2 minutes with a wooden spoon or spatula.

Stand the spoon or spatula straight down into the milk to cause the spinning motion of the milk to stop.

Add the rest of the lemon mixture and stir the spatula in a back and forth motion or a figure eight motion. The intent is to mix the lemon juice coagulant in thoroughly but gently.

After a minute or two, the soy milk should start to separate and curds will begin to form. Stop stirring and cover the pot with a lid.

Let sit for 10 to 15 minutes.

Afterwards, the soy milk will have completely separated into bits of soybean curd and liquid. The Liquid should be rather clear and yellowish. If it is still milky looking, it has not completely curdled. In that case, add a few drops of lemon juice and stir them in well.

Prepare a colander or sieve lined with a few layers of cheesecloth over a bowl, or use a steamer pot.

Ladle the soy curds into the cheesecloth.

Pull up the sides of the cloth to allow most of the water to drain out. Gather the sides of the cloth and twist at the top to squeeze out more water.

Untwist the cloth and re-wrap the curds so that it forms a loaf shape.

With the curds securely wrapped in the cheesecloth, place 5 to 10 pounds of weight on top. The more weight, the firmer your tofu will be. You want to press the curds evenly to force the water out. A cutting board with a few books on top would work well. Alternatively, use a tofu press device.

Let sit for 30 minutes to an hour.

Carefully unwrap the tofu and place in a bowl of very cold water. This will help the tofu firm up further.

Yield: 3 cups
Prep time: 10 minutes
Cook time: 2 hours
Source: Mary's Test Kitchen

Bahamian Style Grilled LOST HER

This recipe is an adaptation of a lobster dish.

1 ½ pounds, 8 small firm tofu steaks
Salt and pepper to taste
2/3 cup very finely chopped onion
2 cloves garlic, minced
½ to 1 bird pepper or other hot chili, minced (to taste)
2 tablespoons fresh lime juice
4 tablespoons (1/2 stick) butter
4 lime wedges for serving

Preheat the grill to high. Cut tofu to ½ inch thick. Season both sides with salt and pepper. Oil the grate. Cook 1 minute per side.

Cut 12 x 8 inch sheets of aluminum foil. Place 1 or 2 small LOST HER steaks on each piece.

Combine onion, garlic, pepper and sprinkle on each steak.

Drizzle each steak with ½ tablespoon lime juice and 1 tablespoon butter.

Fold foil to make an airtight package for each steak. Place on grill 5 minutes. Open packages (watch out for steam), arrange on plates or platter and garnish with lime wedge.

Serves: 4
Prep Time: approx. 15 Minutes.
Cook Time: approx. 5 Minutes.
Adapted from Source: The Barbeque Bible.

Bahamian MA UNHI

This recipe is an adaptation of a Mahi Mahi dish.

2 pounds firm tofu cut into fillet shapes
1/2 cup dark rum
1/2 cup fresh lime juice
2 onions, sliced into thin rings
1 lemon, sliced
2 teaspoons dried oregano
4 tablespoons butter
Ground black pepper to taste

Preheat oven to 350°F. Arrange the fillets in an ovenproof 9x13 glass-baking dish. Pour rum and lime juice over the fillets and place a slice of onion and a slice of lemon on each fillet.

Sprinkle with oregano and black pepper to taste. Place a pat of butter or olive oil on each fillet. Bake, covered, for about 15 minutes.

This is a Bahamian recipe I was given on Bimini many years ago. This goes well with a nice salad, garlic bread and a bottle of good German white wine.

Serves: 4
Prep Time: approx. 10 Minutes
Cook Time: approx. 15 Minutes
Source Allrecipes,

Jerked LOST HER with Coconut

This recipe is an adaptation of a lobster dish.

1½ cup milk
1 cup unsweetened cream of coconut
2 tablespoons Dry Jerk Seasoning
2 pounds firm tofu, cut into chunks
salt and pepper to taste
¼ cup freshly grated Parmesan cheese
8 toast points

Preheat the oven to 400° F.

Mix together the milk and cream of coconut. Heat in a large saucepan over moderate heat. Add the Dry Jerk Seasoning. Stir and cook for about 5 minutes. Add the tofu, (LOST HER) chunks and salt and pepper to taste, and reduce the heat.

Simmer for 7 minutes to blend all the flavors.

Pour the mixture into a baking dish and sprinkle with the grated cheese. Bake for about 15 minutes, until the LOST HER is browned.

The flavor of jerk is delicious mixed with coconut. The sweetness of the coconut balances well with the spiciness of the jerk.

Serves: 4
Prep Time: approx. 15 Minutes
Cook Time: approx. 30 Minutes
Source web: Helen Willinsky

Grilled SALM - UN with Habanero Lime Butter

This recipe is an adaptation of a salmon dish.

Marinade for SALM - UN fillets:
1/4 cup vegetable oil
1/2 cup orange juice
3 tablespoons lime juice
1 tablespoon tequila
1 tablespoon grated lime zest
1 tablespoon minced habanero pepper
1 clove garlic, minced
4 Firm tofu (4 ounce) fillets (SALM – UN)
Habanero Butter (see Sauces)

In a stainless steel bowl or glass baking dish, combine vegetable oil, orange juice, lime juice, tequila, lime zest, habanero, and garlic. Mix well. Place the Tofu SALM - UN fillets into the marinade and coat evenly. Refrigerate for 2 hours. Prepare Habanero Butter and chill.

Preheat an outdoor grill for medium heat, and lightly oil grate. Place tofu SALM - UN fillets on grill, turning once, and basting frequently with marinade. Cook until grill marks appear. Serve with habanero butter on top.

Serves: 4
Prep Time: approx. 15 Minutes
Cook Time: approx. 10 Minutes
Source: Allrecipes

Grilled Spiny LOST HER with Basil Butter

This recipe is an adaptation of a lobster dish.

2 pounds firm tofu (4 LOST HER tails)
8 tablespoons salted butter, melted
Salt and fresh ground pepper
½ cup fresh basil, coarsely chopped
1-2 limes, halved

Preheat the grill to high.
Cut tofu into lobster sized tails. Brush with some of the melted butter and salt and pepper to taste. Add the chopped basil to the remaining butter. Oil the grate.

Arrange the tofu tails on the grill and grill 6-8 minutes. Turn and grill, squeeze lime juice and brush with basil butter.

Serve immediately with remaining basil butter in ramekins on the side.

Serves: 4
Prep Time: approx. 15 Minutes
Cook Time: approx. 10 Minutes
Source: St. Bathelemy Hostellerie de Trois Forces. The Barbeque Bible

Margarita MA UNHI Acapulco

This recipe is an adaptation of a Mahi Mahi dish.

2 pounds firm tofu cut into 1 inch thick (MA UNHI fillets)
1/3 cup Tequila
1/2 cup Triple Sec liqueur
3/4 cup fresh lime juice
1 teaspoon salt
3 cloves garlic, minced
4 tablespoons olive oil
3 tomatoes, chopped
1 onion, chopped
1 jalapeno pepper, seeded and minced
1 pinch white sugar
4 tablespoons chopped fresh cilantro
Ground black pepper to taste

Place cut tofu fillets in a large, shallow dish.
In a small mixing bowl combine tequila, Triple Sec, lime juice, salt, garlic and olive oil. Pour mixture over fillets, and rub into tofu fillets. Cover and refrigerate for 1/2 hour, turning the fillets once.

Heat the grill to a high heat. In a medium bowl, mix together tomatoes, onions, chilies, cilantro, sugar, and salt to taste. Remove fillets from marinade and pat dry. Reserve marinade. Brush the fillets with oil and ground black pepper. Grill fillets for approximately 4 minutes per side.

While the fillets are grilling, boil the marinade in a saucepan for 2 minutes. Remove garlic cloves. Spoon marinade and tomato mixture over the tofu fillets just before serving.

Serves: 6-8
Prep Time: approx. 15 Minutes
Cook Time: approx. 30 Minutes
Source: Allrecipes

CrockPot Jerk Tofu

1 pound firm Tofu
2-4 tablespoons Busha Browne's Authentic Jerk Seasoning
1-cup water
½ lemon
½ lime
4 potatoes
2 carrots

Place in 6 Qtr. Crockpot.
Spread remainder of seasoning over Tofu.
Place on top of Tofu with lime and lemon slices.

Cut potatoes and carrots into smaller pieces and spread around Tofu. Add 1-cup water.
Cover.

Cook on low 4 Hours.

Serves: 4
Prep Time: approx. 15 Minutes
Cook Time: approx. 4 hours
Source: Keevin's Trini Style

Grilled Tofu with Fresh Mango Salsa

2 pounds tofu, sliced ½ inch thick fillets
Salt and freshly ground black pepper to taste
1 tablespoon olive oil
2 cloves garlic, peeled and minced
1 (1/2 inch) piece fresh ginger root, minced
2 mangos - peeled, seeded, and diced
2 tablespoons cider vinegar
1 teaspoon white wine
1/4 cup chopped fresh cilantro

Preheat an outdoor grill for high heat, and lightly oil grate. Rub tofu with salt and pepper. Cook on the grill 4 minutes on each side. Remove from heat, set aside, and keep warm.

Heat oil in a medium skillet over medium heat, and sauté garlic for about 1 minute. Mix in ginger and mangos, and cook 3 to 4 minutes, until mangos are tender. Pour in the cider vinegar and white wine. Season with salt and pepper. Stir in cilantro, and remove from heat.

Spoon over the grilled tofu to serve.

Serves: 4
Prep Time: approx. 15 Minutes
Cook Time: approx. 30 Minutes
Source: Allrecipes

Jay's Grilled Jerk Tofu

6 green onions, chopped
1 onion, chopped
1 jalapeno pepper, seeded and minced
3/4 cup soy sauce
1/2 cup distilled white vinegar
1/4 cup vegetable oil
2 tablespoons brown sugar
1 tablespoon chopped fresh thyme
1/2 teaspoon ground cloves
1/2 teaspoon ground nutmeg
1/2 teaspoon ground allspice
1 1/2 pounds tofu fillets

In a food processor or blender, combine the green onions, onion, chili pepper, soy sauce, vinegar, vegetable oil, brown sugar, thyme, cloves, nutmeg and allspice. Mix for about 15 seconds.

Place the Tofu in a medium bowl, and cover with the marinade mixture. Refrigerate for 2 hours.

Preheat grill, and lightly oil grate. Grill tofu until char lines are set.

Serves: 4
Prep Time: approx. 15 Minutes
Cook Time: approx. 30 Minutes
Source Allrecipes

Key West Grilled Tofu

3 tablespoons soy sauce
1 tablespoon honey
1 tablespoon vegetable oil
1 teaspoon lime juice
1 teaspoon chopped garlic
2 pounds tofu cut into 4 tofu steaks

In a shallow medium dish, blend soy sauce, honey, vegetable oil, lime juice and garlic. Place Tofu steak into the mixture. Marinate in the refrigerator at least 30 minutes.

Preheat grill for high heat and lightly oil grate.

Place marinated tofu on the prepared grill. Cook 6 to 8 minutes.

Serves: 4
Prep Time: approx. 35 Minutes
Cook Time: approx. 30 Minutes
Source: Allrecipes

Lechon Asado: Cuban Shredded Jackfruit

1 1/2 pounds Jackfruit cut into chucks
1 pint water to cover
1 lime, juiced
1 sprig fresh thyme
8 black peppercorns
1 tablespoon garlic powder, or to taste
1 tablespoon onion powder
Salt to taste
2 tablespoons olive oil
1 large onion, halved and thinly sliced
3 cloves garlic, peeled and sliced
1 lime, juiced
1/4 cup chopped fresh cilantro

In a large saucepan, combine water, juice of one lime, thyme sprig, peppercorns, garlic powder, onion powder and salt. Bring mixture to a boil. Add Jackfruit chunks, reduce heat to medium-low and simmer 1/2 hour, until tender. Add water as necessary to keep chunks covered. Turn off heat and let rest in the broth for 30 minutes. Remove from broth and shred, set aside.

In a large frying pan, heat olive oil over medium-high heat. Add the shredded Jackfruit and fry until it is almost crisp, about 5 minutes. Add the onion and garlic and continue to cook until the onion is just tender yet slightly crisp, about 10 minutes more. Add the juice of one lime, mix though and toss with cilantro. Serve and enjoy.

This is traditionally served with black beans and rice.

Serves: 4-6
Prep Time: approx. 15 Minutes
Cook Time: approx. 30 Minutes
Source: Allrecipes

Chapter 9

Breads & Puddings

- Banana and Corn Meal Festival - Jamaica
- Coconut and Sweet Potato Pudding - Jamaica
- Coconut Johnny Cake – All Islands
- Fried Dumplings - Jamaica
- Johnny Cake - Bahamian
- Lemon Pudding - St. Croix
- Mango Bread Pudding with Rum Sauce - Bahamas
- Roti - Jamaica

Banana Corn Meal Festival - Jamaica

2 cups fine cornmeal
½ cup all purpose flour
2 teaspoons baking powder
½ cup dark brown sugar
3 ripe bananas – chopped
1 ½ cups water

Sift all dry ingredients into mixing bowl with chopped banana.

Add water until it becomes light batter.

Heat frying pan with a small amount of vegetable oil.

Spoon 1/6 of batter into pan. Reduce heat to low and cook until it starts to bubble and develops golden brown color at the edge. Flip and cook the other side.

Serve with hot tea.

Serves: 6
Prep time: approx. 5 Minutes
Cook time: approx. 10 Minutes
Adapted from source: Ras Rody Organics

Coconut and Sweet Potato Pudding - Jamaica

3 cups sweet potatoes
2 cups all purpose flour
½ cup dark brown sugar
2 teaspoons baking powder
½ teaspoon baking soda
½ teaspoon cinnamon
1 cup rich coconut milk
2 teaspoons vanilla extract

Sift all dry ingredients into a large bowl.
Grate sweet potatoes on fine grater and add to the dry ingredients.

Slowly incorporate coconut milk until it becomes a light batter.
Stir in the vanilla extract.

Pour the batter into greased and floured 9x9 in cake dish.

Bake for 1 hour or until top browns.

Cool before removing from the baking dish.

Serve with warm coconut sauce.

Serves: 8
Prep Time: approx. 15 Minutes
Cook Time: approx. 60 Minutes
Adapted from source: Ras Rody Organics

Coconut Johnny Cake – All Islands

3 cups all purpose flour
1 tablespoon baking powder
1/3 cup sugar
Pinch of salt
¼ tsp cinnamon
4 tbsp margarine
1 cup coconut milk

Mix flour, baking powder, sugar, salt and cinnamon together in a bowl. With a fork, or using your hand (quick method) rub margarine into flour mixture. Add coconut milk to make a firm dough, but not stiff. Dough should be easy to roll.

Let dough sit, covered for at least an hour.

Roll dough to about 1/4 inch in thickness and cut with a biscuit cutter.

Heat about 3 inches of oil on a medium fire. When oil is hot, fry dough until golden brown, flipping once. Best when served hot.

*Make sure the oil is hot. This makes the dough to puff almost instantly when it hits the hot oil and form a pocket in the middle.

Serves 6
Prep Time: approx. 15 Minutes
Cook Time: approx. 30 Minutes
Source: DL Phelps

Fried Dumplings - Jamaican

1 cup bread flour
½ teaspoon baking powder
2 tablespoons dark brown sugar
½ cup cold water
2 cups coconut oil – warmed until it becomes liquid

Add the coconut oil to bread four, baking powder, and brown sugar. Mix together.

Pour in water and combine with fingers until it reaches soft texture.

Roll firmly into 1" round balls in your hands, ensuring to work the dough.

Allow 1 hour to proof this dough, allowing the baking powder to rise. Heat vegetable oil in a heavy bottomed pot to 350°F.

Drop dumplings into the hot oil and fry until it reaches golden brown color.

Serve with pineapple sauce.

Serves: 6
Prep Time: approx. 15 Minutes
Cook Time: approx. 30 Minutes
Source: DL Phelps

Johnny Cake - Bahamian

½ cup butter, room temperature + extra for greasing pan
¾ cups sugar
4 cups flour
½ cup water
½ teaspoon salt
2 teaspoons baking powder
approx. ¾ cup milk

Preheat oven to 325 °F.

Using an electric mixer beat the butter and sugar together until combined. Add the flour, water, salt, and baking powder to the bowl. Add the milk slowly until the batter is sticky.

Dust hands with flour. Transfer dough from bowl to a greased 9×9 pan. Gently flatten the dough in the pan. Bake for approx. 1hr or until the edges of the johnnycake are browned. The johnnycake will not rise much.

Let cool for several minutes before cutting into the johnnycake.

Serves: 6
Prep Time: approx. 10 Minutes
Cook Time: approx. 60 Minutes
Source: DL Phelps

Lemon Pudding – St. Croix

1 cup self-raising flour
1/2 cup sugar
1 lemon zest only (use the juice in the sauce)
1/2 cup milk warmed
2 tablespoons butter (melted and mixed in with the warm milk)

Sauce:
1/4 cup sugar
1 cup water boiling
1/5 cup lemon juice (2 to 3 lemons)

Pre-heat the oven to 355°F.
Oil a medium sized high-sided baking dish with butter.
Mix together the flour, sugar and lemon zest in a medium bowl.

Pour the milk / butter mixture into the dry ingredients and stir until well combined. Empty the batter into the baking dish.

Mix the sauce ingredients together, then carefully pour over the batter in the baking dish. Bake for about 35 minutes or until the top is golden brown and the sauce starting to bubble around the sides.

Take out of the oven, then leave for 10 to 15 minutes to allow the sauce to thicken slightly before serving.
Sprinkle with icing sugar and serve immediately with vanilla ice cream (if you like).

Serves 6
Prep Time: approx. 10 Minutes
Cook Time: approx. 35 Minutes
Source: DL Phelps

Mango Bread Pudding with Rum Sauce - Bahamas

1/3 cup raisins
4 tablespoons dark rum, split for soaking raisins and sauce
1/2 ounce unsweetened butter
8 cups diced challah

EGG MIXTURE INGREDIENTS:
1 large mango, peeled cored and diced
4 large eggs
2 cups milk
1/4 cup flaked coconut
1/2 teaspoon grated ginger
1/2 teaspoon vanilla extract or 1/2 vanilla bean, scraped from pod
1/2 cup light brown sugar
1 teaspoon cinnamon
1 teaspoon grated nutmeg

RUM SAUCE INGREDIENTS:
3 1/2 ounces unsalted butter
1 cup brown sugar
1 cup heavy cream

GARNISH:
1 tablespoon flaked coconut
mango, slices

Soak raisins in rum for 15 minutes then strain reserving rum for sauce.

Butter a 9x11 casserole pan with 1/2 ounce butter.
Place bread cubes in prepared pan top with raisins.

Process in a food processor the egg mixture ingredients till smooth. Pour over bread, cover with plastic wrap and let soak for 1 hour.

Preheat oven 350°F.

Bake for 40 minutes top with 1 tablespoon coconut and bake 5-10 more minutes.

Meanwhile melt the butter add 1 cup brown sugar and cream stir till dissolved. Add rum that was used to soak raisins.

Serve pudding hot with lots of sauce and garnish with sliced mango.

Serves: 6
Prep Time: approx. 20 Minutes
Cook Time: approx. 60 Minutes
Source: DL Phelps

Roti – Jamaica

1 cup of all purpose flour
2 tablespoon salt
1/2 cup milk
2 tablespoon butter
2 tablespoon sugar
1 tablespoon baking powder

Combine the flour, salt, and baking powder.
Add the water gradually, working the dough into a soft, smooth texture.
Let rest 15 minutes.

Divide the dough into six pieces and shape into round balls, or "loyahs."

Using your fingers, flatten each loyah into a 3-inch disk. Brush each disk on one side with oil and dust with flour. Using a griddle or thick-based frying pan, place two disks together with their oiled sides touching and flatten to 4-inch double disks. Let rest on a floured surface for 10 minutes. Dust a rolling pin and rolling surface with additional flour and roll out into 8-inch disk.

Flip and dust with more flour. Remove excess flour and transfer to the pan or griddle.

Bake on the flat surface until small bubbles appear.
Turn with spatula and brush with oil.
Turn over and brush the other side with oil.
Bake 1 minute.
Fill with curry vegetables.

Serves: 6
Prep Time: approx. 15 Minutes
Cook Time: approx. 5 Minutes
Source: DL Phelps

Chapter 10

Desserts & Cakes

- Carrot Cake - Jamaica
- Coconut Cake – Puerto Rico
- Key Lime Pie – Key West
- Lemon Cake – Key West
- Peach Tart - Bahamas
- Strawberry Cake - Jamaica

Carrot Cake

2 cups all purpose flour
¾ cup dark brown sugar
2 teaspoons baking powder
½ teaspoon baking soda
½ teaspoon all spice
½ teaspoon cinnamon
½ teaspoon salt
5 medium carrots
1 ripe banana
½ teaspoon fresh ginger
¾ cup vegetable oil
¾ cup coconut milk

Preheat oven to 350°F.
Sift the flour, baking powder, baking soda, all spice, cinnamon, and salt into large mixing bowl.

In another mixing bowl mash the banana. Add the sugar and oil to the banana and whisk until light.

Grate carrots and ginger on fine grater and mix with sugar mixture. Gently fold ½ of the dry ingredients into the bowl. Slowly incorporate coconut milk until it becomes light batter.

Gently fold the rest of the dry ingredients into the bowl. Pour batter into greased cake dish and bake for 1 hour or until top browns. Cool before removing from baking dish.

Serve with warm Carmel sauce.

Serves: 6
Prep time: approx. 15 Minutes
Cook time: approx. 60 Minutes
Adapted from source: Ras Rody Organics

Coconut Cake with Pineapple Filling – Puerto Rico

For the Coconut Cake:
2 cups all-purpose flour
1 Tablespoon baking powder
1 teaspoon salt
1/2 cup unsalted butter, room temperature
2 cups granulated sugar
13.5 ounces canned unsweetened coconut milk, divided
1 1/2 teaspoons coconut extract
5 large egg whites

For the Pineapple Filling:
20 ounce can crushed pineapple
2/3 cup granulated sugar
2 Tablespoons cornstarch

For the Coconut Cream Cheese Frosting:
1/2 cup butter, room temperature
8 ounces cream cheese, room temperature
4-5 cups powdered sugar
Remaining coconut milk, or 2 tablespoons regular milk
1 cup shredded sweetened coconut

For the cake:
Line the bottom of two 8 or 9-inch cake pans with wax or parchment paper.

Preheat oven to 350°F.

In mixing bowl, whisk together flour, baking powder and salt. Set aside.

In a separate mixing bowl, beat the butter on medium speed (with hand or stand mixer) for 1 minute, until light and fluffy.
Add sugar and mix 1 minute.
Add 1 1/4 cups coconut milk and coconut extract and mix.

Gradually add flour mixture and mix on medium speed for 2 minutes.

In another bowl, beat egg whites until stiff peaks form.
Fold the egg whites into the batter until incorporated.

Spray the bottom and sides of the lined cake pans with non-stick cooking spray. Divide batter evenly between the pans.

Bake at 350°F. 23-28 minutes, or until a toothpick inserted in the center of the cake comes out clean.

Remove the pans from the oven and allow to cool for 5 minutes before inverting them onto a cooling rack to cool completely. Once cakes have cooled, use a sharp serrated knife cut each cake rounds in half horizontally, so that you end up with four cake rounds.

At this point I like to freeze the cakes for several hours or up to 3 weeks. They're much easier to assemble and frost when they are frozen. But, you can assemble them fresh, the day of.

For the Pineapple Filling:
Add all ingredients to medium saucepan over medium heat. Stir well to combine.

Cook, stirring frequently, until mixture thickens and looks "glossy", about 5-8 minutes.

Pour filling into a tupperware. Place a piece of plastic wrap gently over the top and allow it to cool.
Once cooled, cover it with an airtight lid and refrigerate until you're ready to use it (up to 1 week).

For the frosting:
Beat butter and cream cheese together until smooth.
Add powdered sugar and the rest of the remaining coconut milk (or regular milk). Mix until smooth and fluffy, about 3 minutes.

Add a little more milk, to thin, or powdered sugar to stiffen, if needed, until you reach your desired frosting consistency.
Stir in coconut flakes, saving some for sprinkling on the sides and top of the cake, if desired.

Assembly:

Place your first cake layer on your cake board or serving platter.
Spread half of the pineapple filling over it.
Top with another cake layer. Smooth a layer of frosting over it.
Top with third cake layer. Spread remaining half of the pineapple filling over it.

Top with last (4th) cake round.
Frost the sides and top of the cake. Sprinkle with coconut, if desired.

Refrigerate for at least 4 hours, before serving.

Serves: 6-8
Prep Time: approx. 35 Minutes
Cook Time: approx. 90 Minutes
Source: DL Phelps

Key Lime Pie – Key West

1 cup graham cracker crumbs
3 tablespoons white sugar
5 tablespoons butter, melted
1/2 cup key lime juice
3 eggs
1 pinch salt
1 pinch cream of tartar
1 (14 ounce) can sweetened condensed milk
1 cup heavy whipping cream
1 lime

Preheat oven to 325°F. Mix graham cracker crumbs with sugar and melted butter. Press into 9 inch pie plate and bake for 5 minutes. Remove from oven and let cool. If using bottled key lime juice, measure 1/2 cup of juice. If using fresh fruit, into a measuring cup, squeeze lemons and lime to get 1/4 cup of juice from each.

Separate 2 of the eggs, placing the egg whites into a mixing bowl. Reserve the yolks in another bowl. To the yolks, add one whole egg, 1/2 cup juice and sweetened condensed milk. Mix well. With clean mixer blades, beat the egg whites until stiff, but not dry, adding cream of tartar after about 20 seconds. Fold whites into filling mixture. Pour filling into partially baked crust.

Bake in preheated oven for 10-15 minutes or until set. Let cool at room temperature, then freeze 4 hours to overnight. Just before serving, whip cream to form stiff peaks. Serve decorated with whipped cream and lime slices. You may substitute the key lime juice with a mixture of 1/4 cup fresh lemon juice and 1/4 cup fresh lime juice. Makes 1 - 9 inch pie

Serves: 8
Prep Time: approx. 15 Minutes
Cook Time: approx. 30 Minutes
Source: DL Phelps

Lemon Cake – Key West

1 3/4 cups granulated sugar
2 tablespoon lightly packed finely grated lemon zest
1 ½ sticks butter, room temperature
2 1/3 cups cake flour
1 tablespoon baking powder
1/8 teaspoon table salt
1 cup milk
5 large egg whites, at room temperature
1/4 teaspoon cream of tartar
You'll also need lemon buttercream frosting, lemon curd for filling, and candied lemon zest.

Lemon Layer Cake -
Preheat oven to 350F.

Butter and flour two 8-inch round cake pans.

In a mixing bowl, sift together flour, baking powder and salt. Set aside. In the bowl of an electric mixer, beat together butter, sugar and lemon zest for about five minutes.

Add milk and flour mixture alternately, beginning and ending with the flour, scraping down the sides of the bowl to fully incorporate ingredients.

In a second mixing blow with a hand mixer, beat egg whites and cream of tarter until egg whites form a stiff peak. Add eggs whites to the batter, starting with a quarter of the egg whites, and fold gently together with a rubber spatula. Be careful not to deflate the egg whites.

Divide the batter evenly among the prepared pans and smooth the tops of the batter with a spatula. Bake until a skewer inserted into the center of the cakes comes out clean, about 40 minutes. Rotate pans halfway through to ensure even baking.

Allow cakes to cool in their pans for ten minutes, then invert onto cooling racks to cool completely before filling and frosting. Before filling, cut each layer in half horizontally. This is easiest with a long serrated knife, and by pressing one hand on the top of each layer as you cut. Fill with Lemon Curd, and Frost with Lemon Buttercream.

This cake is easiest to frost by using a 'crumb coat' first. This is simply a very thin layer of frosting applied to the cake, which is allowed to dry or set for about half an hour. This makes the cake easier to frost prettily with a second, heavier layer of frosting, without getting crumbs in the final coat.

Serves: 6-8
Prep Time: approx. 25 Minutes.
Cook Time: approx. 60 Minutes.
Source: DL Phelps

Peach Tart - Bahamas

CRUST:
1/2 cup butter, softened
1/3 cup sugar
1 1/4 cups all-purpose flour
1/2 teaspoon almond extract

FILLING:
3 large (3 cups) peaches, peeled, sliced
1/2 cup sugar
1/4 cup heavy whipping cream
1 tablespoon all-purpose flour
1 large egg
2 tablespoons sliced almonds

Preheat oven to 400°F.
Combine butter and 1/3 cup sugar in bowl. Beat at medium speed, scraping bowl often, until creamy. Add 1 1/4 cups flour and almond extract; beat at low speed until well mixed. Press dough onto bottom and up sides of ungreased 9-inch tart pan with removable bottom. Prick bottom and sides of crust with fork. Bake 15-18 minutes or until light golden brown. Remove crust from oven; arrange peach slices over hot, partially baked crust.
Reduce oven temperature to 350°F.

Combine all remaining filling ingredients except almonds in bowl with whisk. Pour filling mixture over peach slices; sprinkle with sliced almonds. Bake 32-40 minutes or until crust is golden brown and filling is set. Cool completely. Store refrigerated.

Serves: 6-8
Prep Time: approx. 15 Minutes
Cook Time: approx. 60 Minutes
Source: DL Phelps

Strawberry Cake - Jamaica

2 cups white sugar
1 (3 ounce) package strawberry flavored Jello
1 cup butter, softened
4 eggs (room temperature)
2 3/4 cups sifted cake flour
2 1/2 teaspoons baking powder
1 cup whole milk, room temperature
1 tablespoon vanilla extract
1/2 cup strawberry puree made from frozen sweetened strawberries

Preheat the oven to 350 °F.
Grease and flour two 9 inch round cake pans.

In a large bowl, cream together the butter, sugar and dry strawberry gelatin until light and fluffy. Beat in eggs one at a time, mixing well after each. Combine the flour and baking powder; stir into the batter alternately with the milk. Blend in vanilla and strawberry puree. Divide the batter evenly between the prepared pans.

Bake for 25 to 30 minutes in the preheated oven, or until a small knife inserted into the center of the cake comes out clean. Allow cakes to cool in their pans over a wire rack for at least 10 minutes, before tapping out to cool completely.

Serves: 6-8
Prep Time: approx. 10 Minutes.
Cook Time: approx. 30 Minutes.
Source: DL Phelps

Glossary

Caribbean Foods Glossary

Ackee
A handful of islands grow ackee as an ornamental tree, but only Jamaica looks at it as a tree that bears edible fruit. The ackee fruit is bright red. When ripe it bursts open to reveal three large black seeds and bright yellow flesh that is popular as a breakfast food throughout Jamaica. Ackee's scientific name, blighia sapida, comes from Captain Bligh, who introduced the plant to Jamaica from West Africa. Ackee is poisonous if eaten before it is fully mature and because of its toxicity, it is subject to import restrictions and may be hard to obtain in some countries. Never open an ackee pod; it will open itself when it ceases to be deadly. Ackee is sold canned in West Indian markets.
Allspice, Pimienta
Dark-brown berry, similar in size to juniper, that combines the flavors of cinnamon, clove and nutmeg.

Annatto
This slightly musky-flavored reddish yellow spice, ground from the seeds of a flowering tree, is native to the West Indies and the Latin tropics. Islanders store their annatto seeds in oil--giving the oil a beautiful color. Saffron or turmeric can be substituted.

Arañitas
Fried "spiders" made of julienne strips of green plantains.

Arrowroot
Neutral tasting starch extracted from the root of tropical tubers, used as a last-minute thickening agent for sauces.

Bay Rum
The bay rum tree is related to the evergreen that produces allspice. Used to flavor soups, stews and, particularly, blaff, the small dark bay rum berry is called "maleguetta pepper" in the French West Indies.

Beans, Peas
Interchangeable terms for red kidney beans, black beans, black-eyed peas, pigeon peas (gandules), and yellow and green lentils.

Often combined with rice, used in soups and stews or pulped and made into fritters.

Bistec a la Criolla
Marinated steak--typically rump, round or sirloin of beef.

Blaff
A broth infused with whole Scotch bonnet peppers and bay rum leaves in which whole or filleted fish is poached.

Blue Marlin
Jamaicans have little need for imported smoked salmon, as they enjoy their own classy variation from the nearby waters of the Gulf Stream. There's even a world-famous marlin tournament held in Port Antonio each year. The marlin that isn't immediately devoured as streaks is carried off to the smoker, where it takes on a milder salmon like flavor and texture that holds up well when thinly sliced.

Boudin, Black Pudding
Sausage that may include pigs' blood, thyme and Scotch bonnet peppers. Frequently served with souse, a pork dish that can include any part of the pig.

Breadfruit
Breadfruit was also introduced to Jamaica from its native Tahiti in 1793 by the infamous Captain Bligh. The breadfruit is a large green fruit, usually about 10 inches in diameter, with a pebbly green skin and potato-like flesh. Breadfruit are not edible until they are cooked and they can be used in place of any starchy vegetable, rice or pasta. Breadfruit is picked and eaten before it ripens and is typically served like squash--baked, grilled, fried, boiled or roasted after being stuffed with meat. It's even been known to turn up in preserves or in a beverage.

Bunuelos
Similar to crullers, they are made with flour, cassava meal or mashed sweet potato and have fruit fillings like guava and banana.

Callaloo
Spelled half a dozen different ways, this colorful word turns up in Jamaican records as early as 1696. This leafy, spinach-like vegetable is typical prepared as one would prepare turnip or collard greens. This variety of callaloo Amaranthus viridis), better known as Chinese spinach or Indian kale, should not be

confused with the callaloo found in the eastern Caribbean, which refers to the leaves of the dasheen plant.

Carambola, Star Fruit
Tart or acidy-sweet star-shaped fruit used in desserts, as a garnish for drinks, tossed into salads or cooked together with seafood.

Calabaza, West Indian Pumpkin
Terms for a number of large squashes or pumpkins used in island stews and vegetable dishes. Hubbard and butternut squash are similar in flavor and make the best substitutes.

Cassareep
Made from the juice of grated cassava root and flavored with cinnamon, cloves and sugar--this is the essential ingredient in pepperpot, the ubiquitous Caribbean island stew.

Cassava
This tuber is also known as manioc and yuca. A rather large root vegetable with a 6- to 12-inch length and 2- to 3-inch diameter, cassava has a tough brown skin with a very firm white flesh. Both kinds of cassava can appear as meal, tapioca and farina and can be bought ready made as cassava or manioc meal, which is used to make bammie. Sweet cassava is boiled and eaten as a starch vegetable. Bitter cassava contains a poisonous acid that can be deadly and must be processed before it can be eaten. This is done by boiling the root in water for at least 45 minutes discard the water). Alternatively, grate the cassava and place it in a muslin cloth, then squeeze out as much of the acid as possible before cooking. Bitter cassava is used commercially but is not sold unprocessed in some countries.

Cherimoya
Pale-green fruit with white sweet flesh that has the texture of flan. Used for mousse and fruit sauces, the fruit is best when fully ripe, well chilled and eaten with a spoon.

Chili Peppers
Members of the Capsicum genus ranging from medium to fiery hot. Scotch bonnet pepper, the most widely used, can be replaced with serrano, jalapeno or other hot peppers.

Chorizo
Spanish sausage that combines pork, hot peppers and garlic, and is similar to longaniza.

Christophine, Chayote, Cho-cho, Mirliton:
A small pear-shaped vegetable, light green or cream colored, and often covered with a prickly skin. Bland, similar in texture to squash and used primarily as a side dish or in gratins and souffles. Like pawpaw (papaya, it is also a meat tenderizer.)

Coco Quemade:
A pudding similar to flan. Also a base for ice creams and a replacement for creme anglaise.

Coo-coo (or cou-cou):
The Caribbean equivalent of polenta or grits. Once based on cassava or manioc meal. It is now made almost exclusively with cornmeal. Versatile coo-coo can be baked, fried or rolled into little balls and poached in soups or stews.

Coconut:
This member of the palm family, which is native to Malaysia, yields fruit all year long. Coconut is edible in both its green and mature forms. Both the water and the "jelly" of the green coconut find their way into island drinks, and meat from the mature coconut gives desserts a Caribbean identity.

Conch:
These gastropods are a beloved part of the cuisine as far north as the Bahamas and Florida. When preparing conch soup, conch salad or, best of all, spicy conch fritters, you must beat the tough conch flesh into tender submission with a mallet, the flat of a cleaver or a wooden pestle before cooking. The job can sometimes (depending on the recipe) be made easier by using a food processor.

Coriander, Cilantro, Chines Parsley:
Intense, pungent herb that looks like parsley. The seeds are used in curries.

Creole, Criolla:
Creole refers to the cooking of the French-speaking West Indies, as well as to southern Louisiana and the Gulf states. Criolla refers to the cuisine of Spanish-speaking islands. Both terms encompass a melding of ingredients and cooking methods from France, Spain, Africa, the Caribbean and America.

Dhal:
Hindu name for legumes; in the Caribbean, it refers only to split peas or lentils.

Darne:
The Caribbean name for kingfish.

Dasheen
Also known a coco, taro and tannia, dasheen is a starchy tuber that is usually served boiled or cut up and used as a thickener in hearty soups. While considered by some to have a texture and flavor superior to that of a Jerusalem artichoke or potato. Potatoes can often be used as a substitute for dasheen in recipes. Dasheen is often called coco, but coco is actually a slightly smaller relative of dasheen.

Escabeche:
The Spanish word for "pickled." It usually refers to fresh fish (and sometimes poultry) that is fried, then picked in vinegar, spices, hot peppers and oil.

Goat:
Goat meat is eaten with enthusiasm in only a few places in the world, and Jamaica is assuredly one of those places. Some credit immigrants from India who search din vain for lamb to prepare their beloved curry. Finding no lambs, they latched onto the next best thing--and curried goat became a Caribbean classic. Most first-timers find goat milder in flavor than lamb and an excellent substitute for lamb in most recipes. Of course, if you can't find goat, you can substitute lamb.

Guava, Guayaba:
Tropical fruit that has over a hundred species. It is pear-shaped, round and oval; yellow to green skinned, with creamy yellow, pink or red granular flesh; and has rows of small hard seeds. The smell and taste are intense and perfumy. Guava is used green or ripe in punches, syrups, jams, chutneys, ice creams and an all-island paste know as guava cheese.

Hearts of Palm:
Ivory-colored core of some varieties of palm trees.

Hibiscus, Flor de Jamaica, Sorrel:
A tropical flower--not to be confused with the garden-variety hibiscus--grown for it crimson sepal, which is used to flavor dinks, jams and sauces. It is available dried and fresh during the Christmas season.

Jack:
A fish family of over two hundred species, these colorful saltwater fish go by a host of varietal names such as yellowtail, greenback, burnfin, black and amber jack. These delicately flavored fish tend to be large, weighing a much as 150 pounds, and readily available in waters around the world. Tuna and swordfish make good substitutes.

Limes:
Caribbean limes have light yellow skins when ripe, though they are often picked green because they go bad rapidly when ripe. When overripe, they turn yellow and are an excellent source of vitamin C. For this reason, the popularity of these citrus fruits grew with the realization by the British Navy that they cured scurvy. Now limes are one of the most important ingredients in Jamaican sauces and marinades, and are used to perk up dishes from savory to sweet. Chicken and fish turn glorious with a mere squeeze of lime. And beverages, cakes and preserves wouldn't taste the same without it.

Lobster:
In Jamaica, it's the spiny or Caribbean lobster that is found--the same delicious crustacean as the langouste in France, and aragosta in Italy, and the langoasta in Spain. Although the texture of this cooked meat is consider in some to be inferior to that of the Maine lobster, the flavor of the spiny lobster meat more that makes up for the inferior texture.

Malanga, Yautia:
A relative of dasheen or taro, this tuber is prevalent throughout the Caribbean.

Mamey Apple:
The large tropical fruit, native to the New Worked, yields edible pulp that's tangerine in color. With a flavor similar to that of the peach, mammey turns up most often as jam.

Mango
Actually a native of India, this fruit has come to be know as "the fruit of the tropics." Mangoes are used in a variety of ways in the Caribbean. Green mangoes are used in hot sauces and condiments, while ripe mangoes appear in desserts and candies and in drinks. The best varieties of mango are the Bombay, East Indian, St. Julian and Hayden.

Ñame

This giant tuber could be called by any of a variety of different names. The Spanish translation of the word ñame is yam. The outer skin is brown and coarsely textured, while the insided is porous and very moist. The ñame grows to enormous size and is considered to be the "king" of tubers.

Nutmeg

Jamaican cooks are insistent--when cooking their recipes, skip over the pre-ground nutmeg sold in supermarkets and buy the spice whole, grating it only as needed. Nutmeg, the inner kernel of the fruit is more flavorful when freshly grated. The spicy sweet flavor of this aromatic spice makes it an excellent addition to cakes, puddings and drinks.

Okra, Okroes, Bhindi, Lady's Fingers, Gumbo:

This finger-shaped vegetable, green-ridged and three to five inches in length, is fried as a side dish, used as a thickening agent in callaloo or mixed with cornmeal to make coo-coo.

Otaheiti Apple:

Yet another fruit introduced from the Pacific by Captain Bligh, the pear-shaped otaheiti apple ranges from pink to ruby red in color. This fruit is usually eaten fresh, though it can be packed in red wine or turned into a refreshing cold drink.

Papaya

This native of South America is still called ""pawpaw"" by some Jamaicans. The papaya has an orange color when ripe, and it's bland flavor resembles that of a summer squash, making it a nice complement to the shaper flavors of other fruits. Green papaya is often used as an ingredient in chutney or relishes and makes a nice main dish when stuffed. When ripe, it is eaten as a melon, or served in fruit salad. Papaya juice makes a nice drink when sweetened with condensed milk or sugar.

Passion Fruit, Maracudja, Granadilla:

Oval-shaped fruit that has a tough shell and a color range from yellow-purple to eggplant to deep chocolate. The golden-yellow pulp is sweet and tropically exotic, and must be strained to remove the seeds. Used primarily in juices, desserts, drinks and sauces.

Peas:

Jamaicans refer to nearly all beans as "peas." Kidney beans are probably the most popular. Gungo (pigeon) peas have also been a hit since their introduction from West Africa by the Spanish, as have cow peas, black-eyed peas, and butter, lima and broad (also called fava) beans. They are the island's primary source of protein--even more than meat. Smaller peas are used in Rice and Peas while larger-sized peas often appear in savory stews and side dishes.

Picadillo:
Spicy Cuban hash, made of ground beef and cooked with olives and raisins.

Pimento:
Just to keep things interesting, Jamaicans call what the world knows as allspice "Pimento"--a word that elsewhere refers o bell peppers or chiles. The more global name refers to the allspice berry, which has the taste of nutmeg, cinnamon, black pepper and clove. All the same, Jamaicans deserve a big say in this naming, since all but a tiny bit of pimento is grown in Jamaica, the remainder being grown in southern Cuba. Thanks to its embrace by English and Spanish colonist, allspice is used in numerous Jamaican classics, from Escoveitched Fish to Jerk Pork.

Plantain:
Technically a banana-family fruit, but generally regarded as a vegetable. Inedible raw, cooked plantains are served as appetizers or starchy side dishes. The unripe (green), ripe (yellow) and very ripe (dark) plantains are used in Caribbean cooking. They become slightly sweet as they ripen.

Saltfish:
Saltfish is any fried, salted fish, but most often cod. With he increasing availability of fresh fish all over Jamaica, some cooks are moving away from this preserved fish dating back to the days before refrigeration. Still, Jamaicans have a soft place in their hearts for the taste of this salted cod (sold around the world in Italian, Spanish or Portuguese markets under some variant on the name bacalao). Ackee and Saltfish is the preferred breakfast of Jamaicans. When imported saltfish has been unavailable, Jamaicans have been known to make their own from fresh fish.

Scotch Bonnet Peppers
The fiery Scotch bonnet pepper, ranging in colors from yellow to orange to red, is considered the leading hot pepper in Jamaica, though several other varieties have recently been developed. Some peppers are sold whole, others are dried and ground, and still others are processed into sauces, such as Jamaica Hell Fire. If

you can't get your hands (wash them afterward!) on Scotch bonnets, you can substitute habaneros or jalapenos.

Sofrito:
Spanish tomato sauce adapted to the islands, used to enhance roasts and thicken stews or soups.

Sorrel:
Brought from India by way of Malaysia, this unusual plant was introduced to Jamaica by the British soon after 1655. Also known as roselle and appealingly, flor de Jamaica, sorrel always blooms in December, when its deep red flower becomes an unrivaled floral decoration for two to three weeks before it evolves into Jamaica's traditional holiday beverage. At that time, the flower are dried and then steeped in water to make a bright red drink that has a slightly tart taste and is the color of cranberry juice.

Soursop, Corossol, Guanabana:
Elongated, spike-covered fruit, slightly tart and delicately flavored. It is used mainly in drinks, punches, sherbets and ice cream.

Stamp and Go, Baclaitos:
Spicy-hot fritters popular throughout the Caribbean. Methods, ingredients and names vary from island to island.

Star Apple:
An important part of a traditional dessert known a as matrimony, the star apple is a succulent round fruit about the size of an orange. Native to Jamaica and the Greater Antilles, the skin of this fruit is either a shiny purple color or a less eye-catching green. No matter what color, the flesh of the star apple is delicious.

Stinking Toe
Actually a pod that resembles a human toe, this bizarre fruit possesses an evil-smelling and rough exterior. The sugary power inside can be devoured on the spot or turned into a flavorful custard or beverage.

Sugar Apple, Sweetsop:
An interesting challenge to eat, the flesh of the sweetsop is actually a collection of black seeds surrounded by sweet white pulp. The sweetsop is native to the tropical Americas.

Tamarind:
This decorative tree produces brown pods containing a sweet and tangy pulp that's used for flavoring everything from beverages to curries and sauces--including Angostura bitters and Pickapeppa sauce. It is also an important ingredient in Jamaican folk medicine.

West Indian Pumpkin:
A member of the gourd, squash and melon family, this squash is also known as calabaza. Possessing a sweet flavor similar to that of butternut squash, this firm-textured vegetable is commonly found in soups, stews, breads and sweetened puddings. Though hardly the same, the best substitutes for calabaza are Hubbard, butternut and acorn squash.

Yam
Similar in size and color to the potato, but nuttier in flavor, it is not be confused with the Southern sweet yam or sweet potato. Caribbean yams are served boiled, mashed or baked.

Yautía
A member of the taro root family, the yautía is the size of a potato, but more pear-shaped. It has a brown fuzzy outer skin. The flesh is white and slimy and is custard-like when cooked. It is one of the most natural thickeners, used to thicken soups, stews, and bean dishes. There is also a purple yautía which is also called mora.

Yucca
Root vegetable similar in length and shape to a turnip, with scaly yamlike skin. Universally made into flour for breads and cakes, and used as a base for tapioca.

Acknowledgments

Truly it takes a village to accomplish not only great things but also small things like this endeavor. I believe when we work together anything is possible. I am forever grateful to my friends and family who have helped this little obsession become a healthy, tasty reality.

Along the way, not only have I collected recipes. But I've collected many flavor pioneers, recipe testers and I am forever in their debt. First, thanks to Karen Garnett and the Caribbean Bride Cookbook who inspired this endeavor. To Maureen Fannon for endless creative support. Thanks to my writers group friends, Margaret Lashly, Terri Emerson, Pam Merkle, and Jami Deise. And to Grab and Virginia Szenas thank you for efforts, support and critical feedback. To Sandy Daum Walker, for testing recipes restaurant. To my personal taste testers; Edward and Zandra Phelps and my kids Brett and Sonya who knew something was up when I served them veggie dogs as kids.

Inspiration from the islands and other sources of recipes are from recipes.CaribSeek.com from allrecipes.com, southernfood.about.com, The Caribbean Bride, The complete book of Caribbean Cooking, Ortiz, Ras Rody Organics, Sips, Bites & Sweets, Roadside Food Projects. Jamaica, Mary's Test Kitchen and Keevin McIntosh, for their contributions to sharing the joys of Caribbean cooking.

To my patient editor Valerie Kalfrin thanks for you continued support and gentle direction.

May you enjoy sharing these meals with new and old friends around the islands. This discovery has been a great joy in my life that I hope to share with you. Namaste and Rastafari!

DL Phelps

ABOUT THE AUTHOR

DL Phelps

Phelps become enchanted with the world of words and imagination since her childhood. The stories of Beatrix Potter read by a gentile old librarian while sitting beside the large stone fireplace of the local library, was straight out of a fairy tale. She imagined peter rabbit hopping around the garden and all the delights to be found there. Every year her family planted a garden in the backyard and from an early age she took an interest in the magic of growing your own food and delight of a fresh taste of homegrown tomatoes and sweet silver queen corn. Her college years took her to study Film, Fine Art and Fashion at the Universities of Oklahoma and Cincinnati and earned her bachelors degree in Creative Writing and Film Studies from Eckerd College in St. Petersburg, Florida. Her work in the film industry took her to many idyllic island getaways and exotic places around the Caribbean and her love for the delights and flavors of the region expanded. While traveling the search for hearty vegetarian meals was a constant theme and endless discovery.

Printed in Great Britain
by Amazon